LOCAL RED BOOK

TUNBRIDGE WE
TONBRIDGE

CROWBRIDGE · PADDOCK WOOD

C000183785

CONTENTS

Red Books showing the way

Every effort has been made to verify the accuracy of information in this book but the publishers cannot accept responsibility for expense or loss caused by an error or omission.

Information that will be of assistance to the user of the maps will be welcomed.

The representation on these maps of a road, track or path is no evidence of the existence of a right of way.

Street plans prepared and published by ESTATE PUBLICATIONS, Bridewell House, TENTERDEN, KENT. The Publishers acknowledge the co-operation of the local authorities of towns represented in this atlas.

Ordnance Survey® This product includes mapping data licensed from Ordnance Survey® with the permission of the Controller of Her Majesty's Stationery Office.

© Crown Copyright   009-14/08-04   All rights reserved
© Estate Publications   ISBN 1 84192 362 1   Licence Number 100019031

www.ESTATE-PUBLICATIONS.co.uk

Legend

	Pedestrianized / Restricted Access
	Track
	Built Up Area
- - - -	Footpath
	Stream
	River
Lock	Canal
	Railway / Station
●	Post Office
P P+	Car Park / Park & Ride
C	Public Convenience
+	Place of Worship
→	One-way Street
i	Tourist Information Centre
8 8	Adjoining Pages
	Area Depicting Enlarged Centre
	Emergency Services
	Industrial Buildings
	Leisure Buildings
	Education Buildings
	Hotels etc.
	Retail Buildings
	General Buildings
	Woodland
	Orchard
	Recreation Ground
	Cemetery

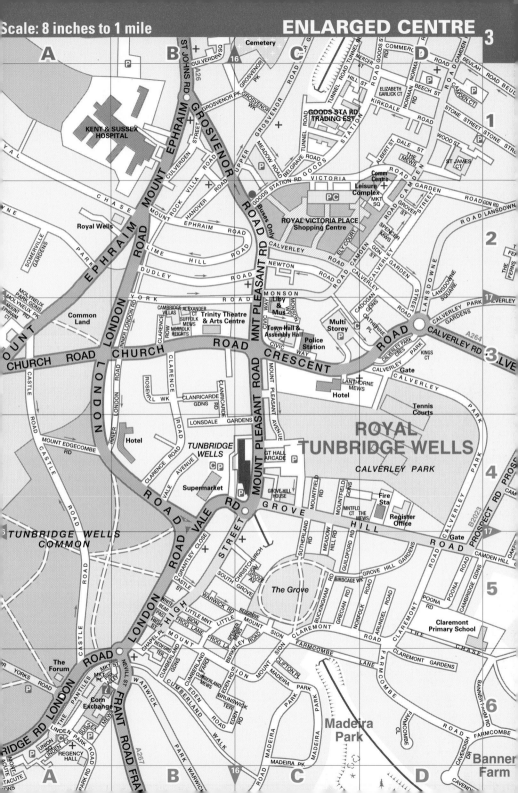

4

A **B** **C** **D**

1

Oakhurst Wood

Cock Wood

HILDENBROOK FARM

LANE

MILL LANE

VINES LANE

RIDING LANE

Alexander House

GARLANDS

2

ROAD LONDON

B245

The Limes Farm

MILL LANE

Great Forge Farm

Hollanden Park Farm

3

A21

Watt's Cross

ROAD

Oak Tree Farm

Flat Wood

WATTS CROSS

St MICHAELS CT

RIDING

Rec Ground

RAPHAEL CT

Raphael Medical Centre

RIDING PK

PARK

RIDING

HARDWICK RD

4

TONBRIDGE

WATTS CROSS ROAD

NOBLE

PHILPOTS LANE

LANE

TREE

Noble Tree Cross

Fosse Bank School

FOXBUSH

ROAD

Playing Field

Sch

Liby

ROAD TONBRIDGE

Sch

RIDING

CHURCH RD

MNT PLEASANT

MNT. PLEASANT

MOUNT PLEASANT

KNOWSLEY

WAY

DERBY CL

FRANCIS RD

COLDHARBOUR

FIDELITY

Oakhill House Fidelity

Hildenborough

HILDENBOROUGH

WEALD CT

Hildenborough Medical Centre

West Wood

LEIGH ROAD

WOODFIELD AV

FIR TREE RO

5

Lucy's Farm

RINGS HILL

Hilden Golf Centre

Club House

HILL

STREET LOWER

STREET

GREEN ROAD

STOCKS GREEN

ROAD

LEIGH ROAD

WILSON CL

FELLOWES WY

School

MEAD W

WEALDEN

ASHLEY ROAD

BYRNES

6

B2027

RINGS HILL BY-PASS

STOCKS

A21

TONE

Bid Bridge

Stocks Green

GREEN ROAD

LEIGH ROAD

BROOKMEAD

BIRCH CL

GREENVIEW CRESCENT

COPSE RD

Hilde Park

A **B** **C** **D**

8

Selbys Farm

E F G H

1

2

3

4

5

6

Cold Harbour Toll

Coldharbour Farm

Roughetts Wood

Coldharbour

COLDHARBOUR LANE

COLDHAR LANE

Stacey's Wood

HORNS LANE

LODGE LANE

Horns Lodge

Pen Stream

Starvecrow Wood

Frogbridge Wood

Trench Farm

COLDHARBOUR

Trench Wood

Hilden Brook

ELMSHURST GARDENS

ASHDEN WK

FERNHOLM WK

WILLOW

ELMSHURST GARDENS

QUINCEWOOD GARDENS

GREENFRITH DR

LINDEN CT

NORTON WK

HEATHER WK

CRESCENT

HAWTHORN WK

SILVERHURST DRIVE

ROWAN SHAW

HAZEL SHAW

SHEAF WY

WHEATSHEAF WY

CORNI

DENBEIGH DRIVE

SHIPB ROAD A227

Madams Toll

School

PINE RIDGE

GREENFRITH DRIVE

BEECHMONT RISE

BISHOPS

OAK RIDE

PLANT

CRESCENT

ST BERNA RDS DR

LARCH CRESCENT

ROWAN SHAW

WHEAT

HARVESTSHEAF DRI

DENBEIGH DR

Little Trench Farm

BRACKEN WK

BISHOPS

TRENCH

NORTHWOOD

OAKMEAD

OAK

BRIAR WALK

YOKE

CLO

PASTORS

RIDE

CORNI WY

DENBEIGH H

High Barn Farm

NORTH TRENCH ROAD

TRENCH ROAD

NEWBOROUGH CT

BRENT CLO

CHASE

PEACH HALL

WHITE COTTAGE RD

Medical Centre

6

Centre for Autism

Sch

WAVENEY ROAD

MEDINA RD

DOVE RD

KENNET RD

TAMAR RD

THAMES RD

MERSEY RD

CLYDE

TWEED

DERWENT

THE BRENT

FOREST GRO

GREENFOLDS CL

CAGE GREEN RD

Cage Green

COVENTRY RD

ST PAULS

COVENTRY RD

ROYAL W

KELLER CL

KENT AV

Schools

TYNE

ROTHER RD

WYE

AVON

ROSPEY

WHITELAKE

THE ACRES

COVENTRY RD

CHATTERLEY CL

SAL

ELY GDNS

Tonbridge Farm Leisure Area

STOUR

COLNE RD

HAMBLE RD

DARENTH WY

FROME CT

SHUNGERS WK

LESLIE TEW CT

SHELTON CL

THORPE AVENUE

C

RIDGEWAY LANE

ROCHESTER

WELLS

EXETER CL

CHEVIOT

Latters Farm House

HILL VIEW ROAD

PARK AV

OAKLANDS

FARM LA

SHERIDAN FARM

STACEY ROAD

Training Ground

LONG MEAD CL

CHERWELL CL

LONG MEAD WY

DERNIER ROAD

MATLAM ROAD

CHILTERN

YARDLEY

Cricket & Football Ground

Rugby Ground

BEAULIEU RD

WELLAND

Cemetery

SHIPBOURNE ROAD

EXETER

RD

TONBRIDGE ROAD

LONDON ROAD

GROVE

HAWDEN CLOSE

PARK ROAD

HILDEN

HILDEN

CLOSE

HILDEN PARK ROAD

Hilden Manor

High Hilden House

COURT LANDS

Tonbridge Oast Theatre

B245

Hotel

HILDEN

School

PARK ROAD

HILL

A227

SHIPBOURNE ROAD

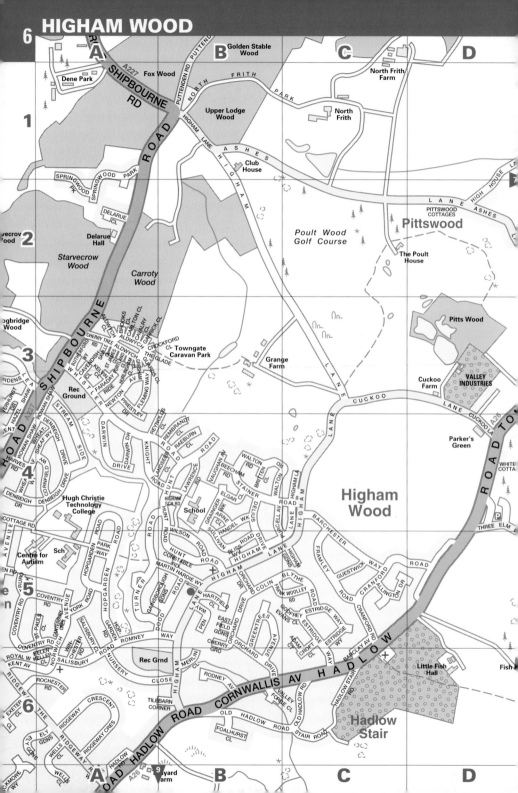

Golden Stable Wood

North Frith Farm

Dene Park

Fox Wood

Upper Lodge Wood

North Frith

PITTSWOOD COTTAGES

Pittswood

Springwood Pk

Delarue Cl

Delarue Hall

Starvecrow Wood

Carroty Wood

Club House

Poult Wood Golf Course

The Poult House

Pitts Wood

Cuckoo Farm

VALLEY INDUSTRIES

Towngate Caravan Park

The Glade

Grange Farm

Rec Ground

Parker's Green

WHITE COTTA

Hugh Christie Technology College

School

Walton Rd

Britten

Stainer

Higham Wood

THREE ELM

Centre for Autism

Sch

Hartfield

Little Fish Hall

Fish

Rec Grnd

Tilebarn Corner

Foalhurst Cl

Hadlow Stair

ayard arm

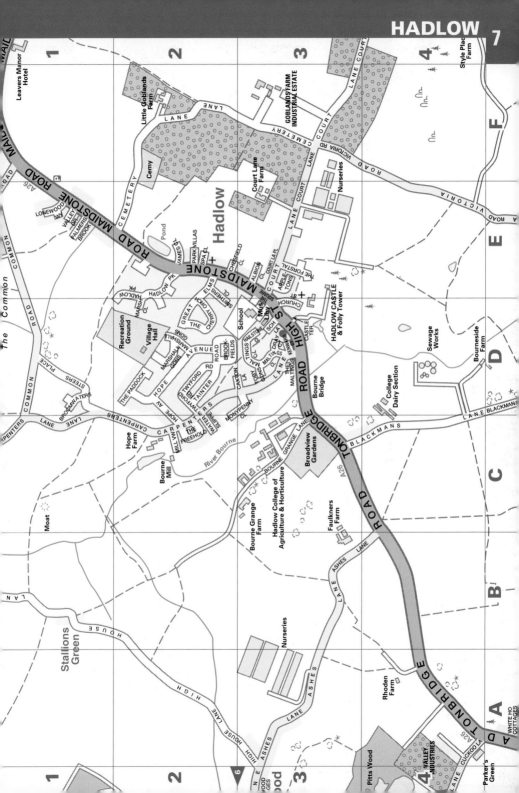

Style Place Farm

Leavers Manor Hotel

Little Goblands Farm

GOBLANDS FARM INDUSTRIAL ESTATE

LANE

Cemy

Cemetery

LANE COURT

Court Lane Farm

Nurseries

Pond

CEMETERY

Hadlow

PARK VILLAS
JAMES ST
SPA CL
CHERFIELD CL
ALBION
CL
COURT LA PL
THE FORSTAL

MAIDSTONE ROAD
A26

LONEWOOD
WY
VALLEY DR
PALMERS BROOK

The Common

COMMON ROAD

STEERS PLACE

BROOKWATERS LANE

CARPENTERS LANE

CARPENTERS LANE

HADLOW PK
MARSH RD
GREAT ELMS
GDNS
SMITHERS CL
THE
FERRY ORCH
MARSHALL GDNS
HOPE AV
TWYFORD
AVENUE
SUTTER
PAINTER
RS
CARPM
THE FREEHOLD
WILL
TWYFORD

Recreation Ground

Village Hall

The Paddock

School

BROOK
FIELDS
ROAD
HAILSTONE LA
THE MALTINGS
CAXTON LA
ORBY
DRAY LA
KENNEDY
THE MALTINGS
DRAY LA
MONYPENNY CL

MAIDSTONE

HIGH

SQUARE

CHURCH ST

HADLOW CASTLE & Folly Tower

CASTLE FER

VICTORIA RD

VICTORIA ROAD
A26

Sewage Works

Bourneside Farm

Bourne Bridge

College Dairy Section

Hope Farm

Bourne Mill

River Bourne

Moat

BOURNE
GRANGE LANE

Broadview Gardens

TONBRIDGE ROAD

BLACKMANS LANE

BLACKMANS LANE

Bourne Grange Farm

Hadlow College of Agriculture & Horticulture

Faulkners Farm

A26

LAN

HOUSE

HIGH

Stallions Green

Nurseries

ASHES LANE

HIGH HOUSE LANE

ASHES LANE

ASHES LANE

TONBRIDGE ROAD
A26

Rhoden Farm

Pitts Wood

Parker's Green

WHITE HO COTTAGES

VALLEY INDUSTRIES

CUCKOO LA

WOOD

GES

NE

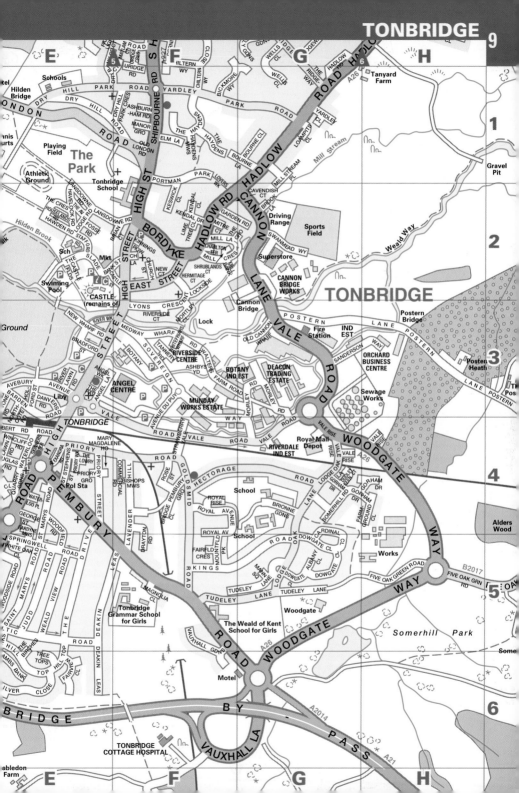

TONBRIDGE

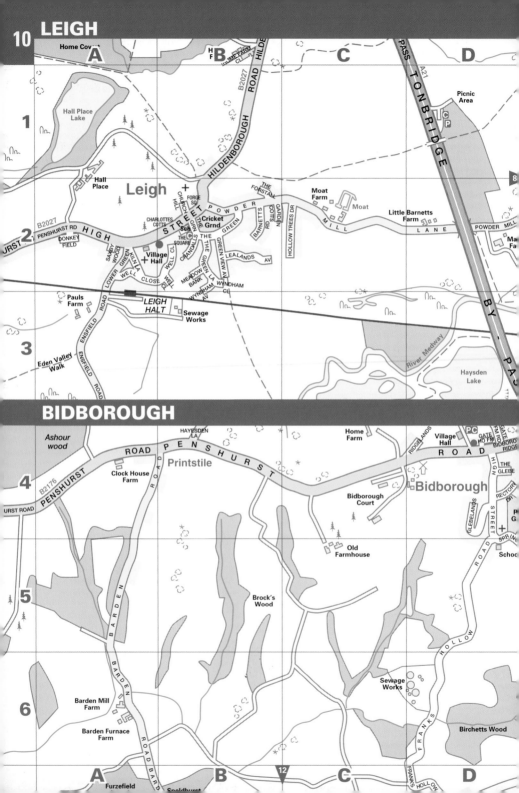

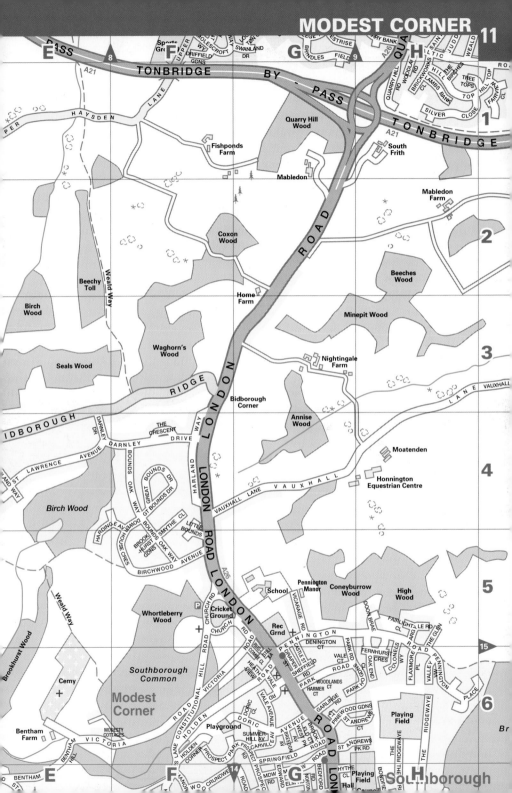

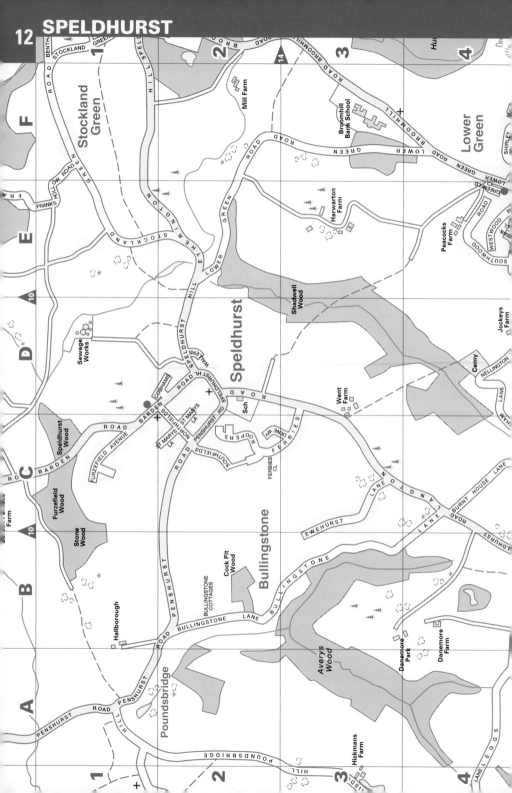

Appletree Wood

Devil's Gd

E **F** **G** **H**

1

Old Forge Farm

Brokes Mill Farm

North Farm

GUARDIAN BUSINESS PARK

KING STANDING

KING STANDING BUSINESS PARK

Forge Farm

Refuse Tip

Brokes Wood

Household Waste Recycling Depot

Sewage Works

GREAT LODGE RETAIL PARK

Superstore

ROAD LONGFIELD

2

DOWDING

WAY

LONGFIELD

LANE

KNIGHTS

Depot

ROYAL TUNBRIDGE WELLS BUSINESS PARK

COLEBROOK IND EST

MUL-BERRY

JUNIPER CL

AVENUE

ALDER WY

ASPEN WY

BLACKHORN

AVENUE

HORNBEAM

WALNUT WAY

LAMBERSWAY CL

STAG

NORTH FARM IND EST

BUSINESS PARK

WAY

KNIGHTS

PARK

KNIGHTS PARK LEISURE COMPLEX

18

BARNETTS

POWDER MILL LA

MILLON WY

HORIZON WY

BARNETTS WY

CHAPMAN WY

HIGH BROOMS INDUSTRIAL PARK

SPA IND PK.

Home Farm

Cinema

3

Spectrum Ho

WEIRE RD

SALISBURY RD

ANDREW

GREAT BROOMS RD

CHAPMAN WY

ORCHARD BUSINESS CENTRE

CHAPMAN WY

NTH FARM RD

APPLE TREE LANE

LAMBERTS WAY

HOME

LONGFIELD

Bowling Alley

Robingate Wood

High Brooms

MILLA POWDER LA

WERRE RD

NURSERY RD

HILL VIEW ROAD

COLEBROOK

WELBECK AV

HIGHFLD RD

NORTH FARM ROAD

Century Place

Playing Field

CLIFTON COTTS

SHENDEN WALK

GRN-HORN

HAZELWOOD

OAKWOOD

WILLOW WY

GREEN WAY

Robin Gate

BLACKHURST

HIGH

GORDON RD

WOLSELEY RD

STEWART RD

HIGHLANDS RD

CAMBRIAN ROAD

HIGH BROOMS

CLIFTON

BROOK

CALEY

RANKINE ROAD

TREBILCO

LONGVIEW WY

LAUREL RD

BRAMBLE WK

WILTSHIRE WY

THEODORE CL

GREGGS

WOOD GREEN

OAKWOOD

LINK

RISE

MIDDLE WY

KEMBLE

4

MERRION CL

MERRION CL

WOODLAND LAND CL

DYNEVOR RD

DENBIGH ROAD

SANDHURST

NTH FARM

OAK END RD

LAUREL RD

HILLCREST RD

RYMERS

BRAMBLE WK

WILTSHIRE WY

MILTON DR

ORCHID HURST LA

BIRCH

THE THISTLE

WOOD

ROAD

Robin Gate

Sch

ROAD

SILVERDALE LA

GROSVENOR RD

QUARRY

BLAKE WAY

BROOK LANDS

DILLDN WY

ORCHARD CL

GLEN-R DALE

LIPTRAPS LA

BIRCHEN RD

LIPTRAPS LA

HARRIES

ALLANDALE

ROAD

BURSLEM

WOOD

ROAD

SILWOOD CL

ROAD

LAKESIDE WAY

Gregg's Wood

MALTON

SWALLOW DR

SANDOWN

A WAVERLEY

SANDOWN GRO

THE RIDINGS

18

ST PEMBURY RGE

HSE HOUSE

5

Hilbert Recreation Ground

HILBERT

RAVENSWOOD

FAIRFIELD AV

PINEWOOD RD

Sherwood

BIRKEN ROAD

FRIARS

BEECHES

School

RED LEAF

GREGG'S HOLT

CEDAR RIDGE

SHERWOOD

ROAD

Sherwood Park

CONEYBURROW RD

HAVENG CL

OSPRINGE PL

THORNFIELD GDNS

Tunbridge Wells High School

Seven Springs Home

Sandown Pa

A264

6

ST JAMES RD

TRAFFORD RD

VENOR ST

WESTERN RD

AUCKLAND RD

DORKING RD

ORCHDALE RD

AXON

STANHOPE

AUCKLAND RD

ST JAMES PARK

KG GEORGE V

RAVENSWOOD AV

SPRINGHEAD

FERNDALE ROAD

FERNDALE

BRACKEN RD

CORSEFIELD

FAIRMILE RD

GORSE RD

SHERWOOD

COHELWOOD

BADGERS

SANDOWN

SANDOWN

HALLS HOLE RD

ROAD PEMBURY

Blackhurst

PEMBURY

CORNFORD

ORCHANDOS

GRANVILL

ALBION RD

ST JAMES PK

ST JAMES ST

ALBAN

HILBERT RD

HUMBO RD

CLEVE LAND

ANDREWS BREW HORD

GRAMPION

FERNDALE

SHERWOOD ROAD

SQUIRREL

CORNFORD

Sch

BEULAH

FERNDALE

MENTMORE

FOSSDALE

PENLEY

AND PENNINE WK

QUANTOCK

NDHIP

17

E **F** **G** **H**

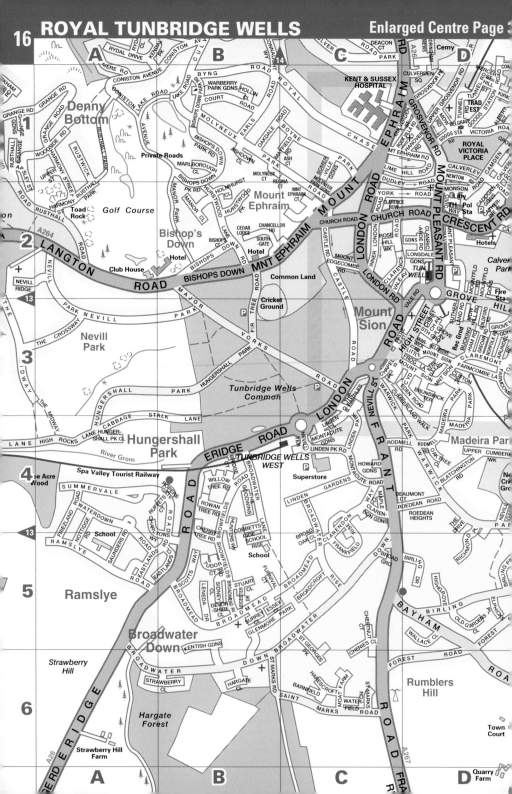

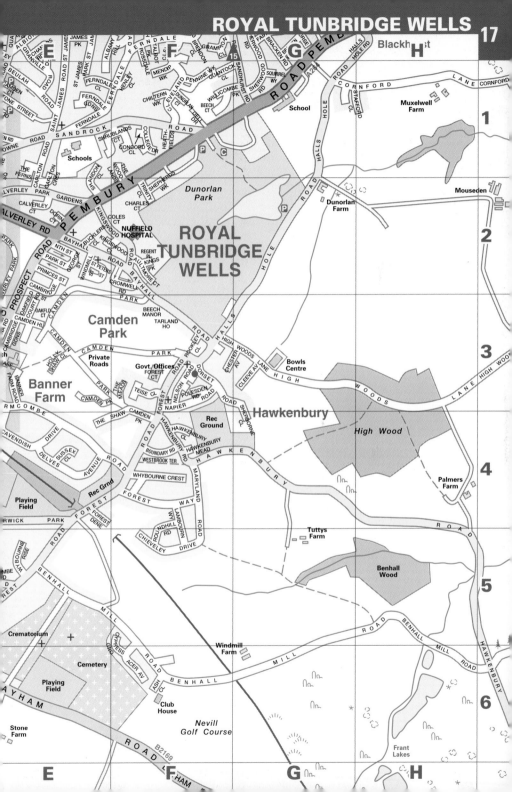

Blackhurst

ROYAL TUNBRIDGE WELLS

Dunorlan Park

Muxelwell Farm

School

Mouseden

Dunorlan Farm

NUFFIELD HOSPITAL

Schools

Camden Park

Private Roads

Govt. Offices

Banner Farm

Bowls Centre

Hawkenbury

High Wood

Palmers Farm

Rec Ground

Tuttys Farm

Playing Field

Rec Grnd

Benhall Wood

Crematorium

Cemetery

Windmill Farm

Playing Field

Club House

Stone Farm

Nevill Golf Course

Frant Lakes

1
2
3
4
5
6

Wadhurst

Pell Green

Great Pell Oast

Primmers Green

Pell Bridge

Turners Green

Osmers Hill

Turner's Green

Playing Field

Sparrow's Green

Vicarage Green

School

Fire Sta

Stone Cross

Uplands Community College

Cricket Ground

Lib

Post Sta

Wadhurst Castle

Stone Bridge

Training Centre & College

Durgates

Durgates Ind Est

Bassetts Forge

School

Windmill Farm

Windmill Wood

Rockrobin

WADHURST

WADHURST BUSINESS PK

Mount Farm

The Mount

Homefield Farm

Ravensdale Farm

Lorien Arboretum

Bellerbys College

Best Beech Hill

Labels (top to bottom, left to right):

Home Wood

FOREST FOLD COTTS
HOADLEYS LA

London

Beeche

Mardens Hill

Keywards Wood

SMUGGLERS LANE

Cook's Corner Farm

Bunkers Hill

SCHOOL LA

INHAMS

NORBURY CL
VIEW ROAD
BEECHES CL
COMMON WOOD
PLEASANT
JEFFRIES WY
JEFFRIES
GILLRIDGE GREEN

Sch
HILL

BROOK VW
COOPERS WOOD
ELIM COURT GDNS
WEST WY
WEST ELLISON WY
SLEIGH LA
RISE

St Johns

Horder Arthritic Centre

SAINT JOHNS ROAD
COOPERS LANE
GHYLL
FAIRVIEW LA
FAIRVIEW COTTS

Goldsmiths Leisure Centre & Recreation Group

PINEWOOD CHASE
CHASE
AVENUE
GOLDSMITH
KINGS
BADGERS CL
ST JOHNS GDNS
THE CLOSE
BRYANTS FLD
BEACON
PILMER

High Cross Fields

P

GLENMORE RD OLD
GLENMORE ROAD EAST
GOLDSMITH AV
SHEILING RD
HIGHLANDS CL
BEACON

Ocklye House

ROAD ERIDGE ROAD
Fire Sta
Council Offices
FERNBANK CENTRE
High St
Broadway
NEW PARK CLO
PARK CRES
NEVILL RD
CROHAM CRES
MILL
LA
WEALDEN

Crowborough

FIELDEN
RANNOCH RD
AVIEMORE
ROAD
INGLESIDE DR
ROAD WEST
BEACON
MILL
GROVE
OLD MILL CT
ASHDOWN
KINGS CT
SAXONBURY
THE MDWS
GRAYCOAT
LOWER SAXON BURY
CLOSE
THE PARK
DR

Crowborough Warren

FOREST PARK
THE DRIVE
AVIEMORE RIDGE
KNOWLE PK
WARREN PK
WELLESLEY CL
WOODSIDE
WILDERNESS PK
BEACON CLOSE
LANE
CROFT
SAXONBURY
CLIFFORD ROAD
WESLEY MWS
JARDINE CT
CHURCH ROAD
GORDON RD
THE GREEN
GLEBELAND

RANNOCH RD WEST
WARREN RD
WARREN GATE
SYNT
HOLLY LA
GRANGE CL
STARFIELD
CHURCH ROAD
COURTLANDS
MYRTLE
VALLEY VW CL
MONTARGIS
HYDEHURST

HEAVEGATE
WARREN ROAD
MELFORT ROAD
MELFORT RD
TWYFORDS
WINDSOR CL
SWIFT CL
LITTLE PADDOCKS
THE TWITTEN
THE GROVE
HOSP & Amb Sta
SANDRIDGE
BUTLER CL
SOUTHVIEW
RISE
WHITEHILL CL
TRENCHES
EDWARD RD
QUEENS
NYE CL
LITTLE
BLACKNESS RD

School

HEAVEGATE ROAD
FIELDEN
BEACON ROAD
SOUTHVIEW ROAD
PRATTS FOLLY LA
HARLEQUIN
SOUTHRIDGE
HARECOMBE RISE
ROHARECOMBE RD
HARECOMBE RD
GLADSTONE RD
FERMOR ROW
STONEX COTTS

FOREST LODGE
LANGTON
SOUTHVIEW
MHINGCROFT PK
Club House
LORDSWELL LANE
HARLEQUIN LANE
HARLEQUIN PL
WILLOW MEAD
MANOR WY
COMBE END
SPRINGHEAD WY
SOUTHRIDGE RISE
COMBE WY
HERNE
COLD HARBOUR COTTS
Cemetery
Sch

WOODLANDS
NEVILL CL
NEVILL CL
Little Warren Farm

Crowborough Trail Camp

BEACON RD
SHEEP PLAIN

Crowborough Common

SHEEP PLAIN

Whitehill

HURTIS HILL
JRTIS LA
HIGH
HURTIS

SWAYLANDS
ALICE
AV

22

E **F** **G** **H**

Hodge's Wood

Burnt House Wood

Cherrytree Farm

1

Cage Wood

A26

ERIDGE ROAD

Golf Course

Club Ho

Limekiln Wood

2

Hourne Farm

ERIDGE ROAD

Playing Fields

ERIDGE LANE

Steel Cross Farm

Camping & Caravan Site

ERIDGE

Steel Cross

Luxford Farm

Limekiln Forest

THE FARTHINGS

MILLBROOK ROAD

OAKHURST DR

ROAD

PELLINGS RISE

Pelling's Wood

PALESGATE LANE

LIMEKILN LANE

Park Wood

3

CHARITY FM WY

HOOKSWOOD CL

GARDENS

ONGTON RD

MILLBROOK ROAD

BARNFIELD

Beacon Community College

PELLINGS FARM CL

POUNDFIELD FARM

Jeffery's Wood

CHEQUERS

CROWBOROUGH

Playing Field

POUNDFIELD ROAD

SPRINGFIELD CL

GREEN LANE

POUNDFIELD FARM

Poundfield

4

College

EAST BEECHES RD

BEECHES ROAD

HILLRISE

SHAW FIELD

MEDWAY WY

ROCHESTER WY

Sch

NORTH BEECHES RD

WEST BEECHES ROAD

SHEPHERDS WK

MEDWAY

Police Sta

OLIVER CL

DOWNSHILL

BEAVER CL

MONTARGIS WAY

WILDERS FARM CL

ASHLANDS

OAKLANDS WY

ROCHESTER WAY

M E D W A Y

5

BEECHES FARM ROAD

BULLER

WALLIS WAY

SIMONS

BOOKER CL

HILL CROWBOROUGH

B2100

ROCHESTER ROAD

RO'WELL

BRACKEN CL

BROOK CL

FOREST RISE

FOREST

HEATHER

WALK

DENE

PALESGATE LANE

MONTARGIS WAY

LOXFIELD GDNS

BURDETT ROAD

School

ROAD

KEMPS FARM

ROCKINGTON WY

TOLLWOOD RD

TOLLWOOD

Country Park

ST MICHAELS CL

ROSEHILL

OSBORNE HILL

WINDSOR RD

VICTORIA RD

Rec Ground

LEXDEN LODGE IND EST

Jarvis Brook

Ford

BLACKNESS

LUXFORD

Recreation Ground

BELVEDERE GDNS

LUXFORD ROAD

BLACKNESS ROAD

OSBORNE RD

RIVERSIDE GDNS

COLLIER MEWS

STATION ROAD

MAYNARDS MEAD

MILLBROOK IND EST

B2100

ROAD

6

Blackness

LINCOLN WY

LUXFORD DR

FARNINGHAM

CROWBOROUGH

DAIRY GRN

KNOWLE CL

ROTHERFIELD

WESTERN GDNS

ROTHERHILL

MOTTINS HILL

TUBWELL LANE

TREBLERS

CLACKHAMS LA

FERMOR

MINT PLEASANT

INDUSTRIAL ESTATE

WEALDON IND EST

22

RD WESTERN

BSNS PK

E **F** **G** **H**

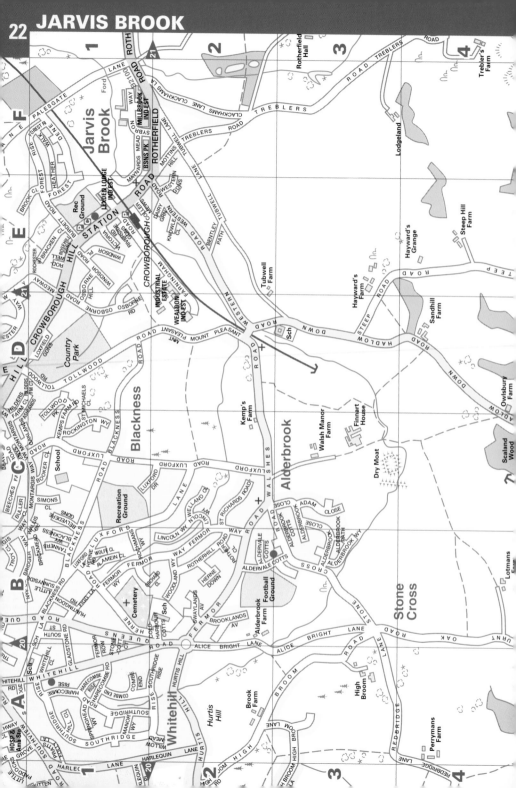

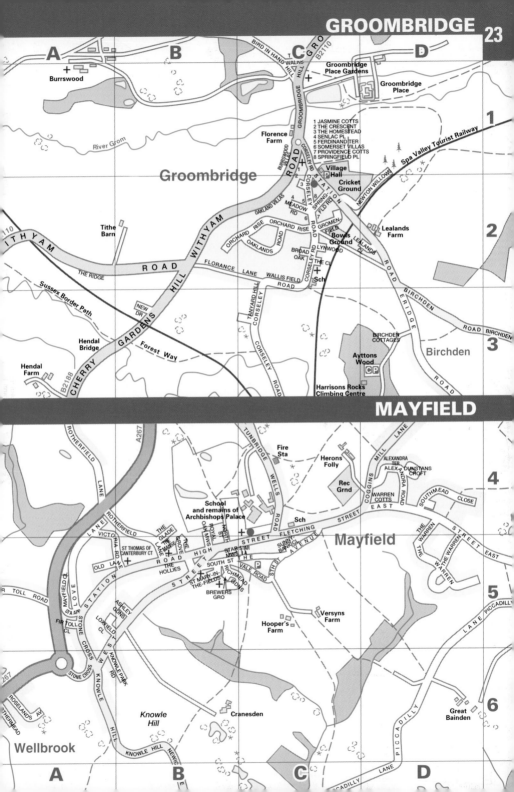

Burrswood

River Grom

Groombridge

B2110

Bird in Hand Walks

HILL GRO

Groombridge Place Gardens

Groombridge Place

Florence Farm

1 JASMINE COTTS
2 THE CRESCENT
3 THE HOMESTEAD
4 SENLAC PL
5 FERDINANDITER
6 SOMERSET VILLAS
7 PROVIDENCE COTTS
8 SPRINGFIELD PL

Spa Valley Tourist Railway

Newton Willows

Village Hall

Cricket Ground

GROOMBRIDGE ROAD

BIRCHWOOD

CORSELEY RD

STATION

SPRING-FIELD RD

OAKLAND VILLAS

MEADOW RD

ORCHARD RISE

ORCHARD RISE

ORCHARD ROAD

Tithe Barn

OAKLANDS

HILL WITHYAM ROAD

ROAD

FLORANCE LANE

WALLIS FIELD ROAD

GROMEN-FIELD ROAD

Bowls Ground

LYNWOOD

BROAD OAK

THE CL

Sch

Lealands Farm

LEALANDS CL

WITHYAM ROAD

BIRCHDEN ROAD

THE RIDGE

Sussex Border Path

NEW DR

CHERRY GARDENS

Forest Way

CORSELEY ROAD

TANYARD HILL

CORSELEY

CORSELEY ROAD

BIRCHDEN COTTAGES

Ayttons Wood
CP

Birchden

ROAD BIRCHDEN

Hendal Bridge

Hendal Farm

B2188

Harrisons Rocks Climbing Centre

ROAD

A267

ROTHERFIELD LANE

Fire Sta

TUNBRIDGE WELLS ROAD

Herons Folly

Rec Grnd

COGGINS MILL LANE

Alexandra Ter
ALEX-ANDRA ROAD

DUNSTANS CROFT

WARREN COTTS

Southmead Close

ROTHERFIELD LANE

VICTORIA RD

THE GLADE

THE MANOR

THE GROVE

OAK MEWS

ROYAL OAK

NORTH STREET

School and remains of Archbishops Palace

Sch

FLETCHING STREET

STREET EAST

Mayfield

OLD LANE

ROAD

THE HOLLIES

HIGH STREET

STAR STAR MWS

SOUTH ST

SUNNY BANK

THE VALE ROAD

ST ST AVENUE

STH ST

THE WARREN

THE WARREN

THE WARREN

LANE PICCADILLY

ST THOMAS OF CANTERBURY CT

Mayfield Ct

LOVE LANE

STATION RD

STA APP

FIR TOLL CL

STONE CROSS RD

ASHLEY GDNS

LONGFIELD CL

KNOWLE PARK RD

ST MARY-IN-THE-FIELDS

RICHMOND GDNS

BREWERS GRO

Hooper's Farm

Versyns Farm

TOLL ROAD

ROSELANDS AV

THERMEAD

Wellbrook

KNOWLE HILL

Knowle Hill

Cranesden

NEWING

PICCADILLY LANE

Great Bainden

A267

1
2
3
4
5
6

A B C D

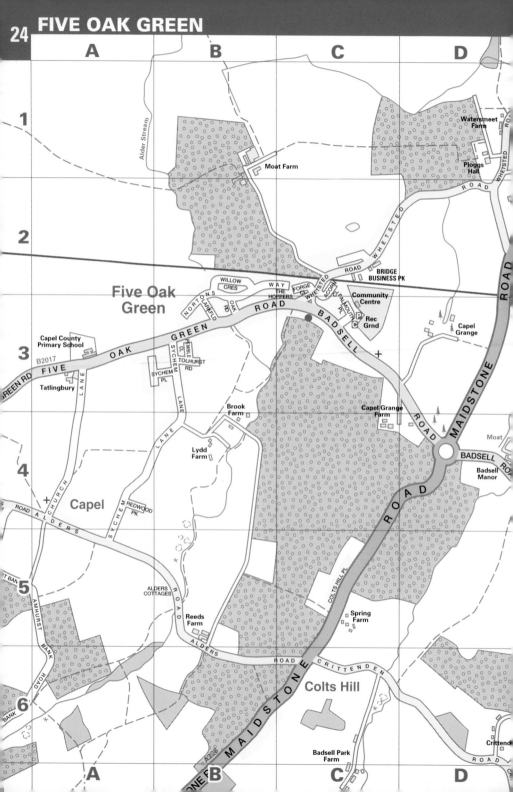

A   B   C   D

1

2

Alder Stream

Moat Farm

Watersmeet Farm

Ploggs Hall

WHETSTED ROAD

BRIDGE BUSINESS PK

Five Oak Green

WILLOW CRES
WAY THE HOPPERS
FORGE CL
WHETSTED ROAD
ACORN
FALMOUTH PL
Community Centre
Rec Grnd

NORTONS
LARKFIELD RD
OAK RD

Capel Grange

Capel County Primary School

3

B2017
FIVE OAK GREEN RD

LANE

SYCHEM LANE
PEMBLE CL
TOLHURST RD

SYCHEM PL

Tatlingbury

BADSELL ROAD

Capel Grange Farm

Brook Farm

Lydd Farm

4

CHURCH ROAD
ALDERS ROAD

Capel

SYCHEM LANE
REDWOOD PK

LANE

ROAD
MAIDSTONE

Moat

BADSELL

Badsell Manor

BADSELL RD

5

ST BANK
AMHURST BANK
ROAD

ALDERS COTTAGES

ROAD ALDERS

Reeds Farm

COLTS HILL PL

Spring Farm

6

BANK

ALDERS ROAD

CRITTENDEN

Colts Hill

MAIDSTONE ROAD
A228

Badsell Park Farm

Crittend

ROAD

A   B   C   D

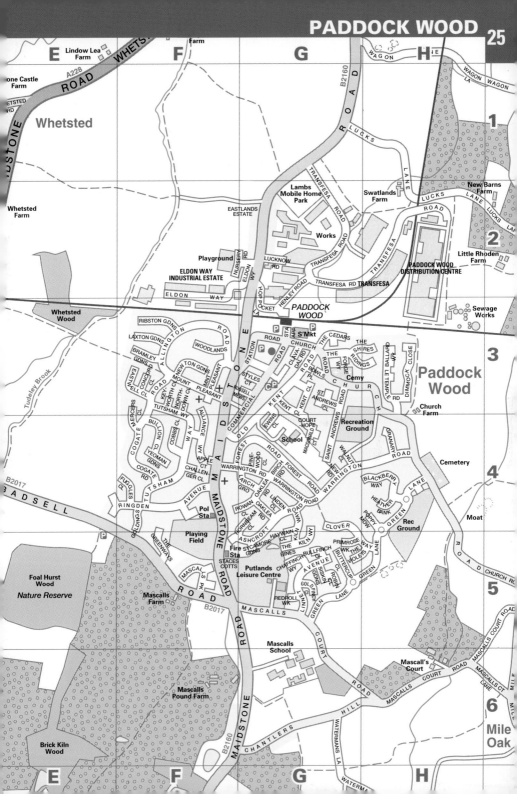

Lindow Lea Farm
Farm

WHETS...
ROAD A228

one Castle Farm
...STED RD

Whetsted

WAGON
WAGON LA
WAGON

B2160

Whetsted Farm

R O A D

LUCKS

LANE

LUCKS LA
LUCKS ROAD

New Barns Farm

1

Lambs Mobile Home Park

TRANSFESA ROAD

Swatlands Farm

2

Little Rhoden Farm

EASTLANDS ESTATE

Works

LUCKNOW RD

TRANSFESA ROAD

TRANSFESA RD TRANSFESA

Playground

ELDON WY

NURSERY RD

PADDOCK WOOD DISTRIBUTION CENTRE

ELDON WAY INDUSTRIAL ESTATE

ELDON WAY

HOP POCKET

PADDOCK WOOD

Sewage Works

Whetsted Wood

RIBSTON GDNS

STA APS

S'Mkt

THE CEDARS

THE SHIRES

THE RIDINGS

DIMMOCK CLOSE

Paddock Wood

3

LAXTON GDNS

WOODLANDS

CHURCH

CLIVA...

DALTRY

THE BOWLS

FOREST

BRYTLE BALE TEMPLE

BRAMLEY GDNS

ALLINGTON ROAD

NEWTON GDNS

MINT PLEASANT

STYLES

ROAD

KENT

KENT CL

ST ANDREWS CL

THE
Cemy

CHURCH ROAD

Church Farm

MOUNT PLEASANT

RUSSELL MEWS

EWINS CL

COURT HOPE

SAINT ANDREWS ROAD

Recreation Ground

GRANARY ROAD

Cemetery

4

EASN...ELL CL

CONCORD ROAD

KEY-WORTH CL

DOWN CL

TUTSHAM WY

OLD

COMMERCIAL

School

MACDONALD CL

WALNUT WY

BLACKBERRY WAY

LANE

Moat

COGATE MEWS

BULLION CL

COBBS RD

ALLIANCE WAY

FOREST ROAD

PINE-WOOD

BIRCH

FOREST ROAD

HENLE...

HEATHER BANK

GREEN

Rec Ground

YEOMAN GDNS

APPLE CT

CHALLEN-GER CL

WARRINGTON ROAD

LARCH GRO

WARRINGTON ROAD

WARRINGTON

POPPY MDW

CLOVER

B2017

BADSELL

COGATE

FUGGLES CL

TUTSHAM

RINGDEN

AVENUE

THE GREENWAYS

MAIDSTONE

Pol Sta

ROWAN CL

OAKLEA

LINDEN ROAD

MAYM...

PRIMROSE WAY

GREEN LANE

ROAD

CHURCH RD

5

GISINGS

Playing Field

MASCALLS PK

CORNBEAM RD

OAKLEA CL

ASHCROFT

HAYWAIN

THE KILN

BINES

BULLFINCH

BUTTERCUP

ROBIN CL

VIOLET

Foal Hurst Wood

Nature Reserve

Mascalls Farm

ROAD

Fire Sta

STACES COTTS

SYCAMORE GDNS

CHAFFINCH

Putlands Leisure Centre

SISKIN

AVENUE

GOLDFINCH

VY

GREEN LANE

MASCALLS CT LANE

MILE

MASCALLS COURT ROAD

Mascall's Court

MASCALLS

REDPOLL WK

LINNET

COURT ROAD

B2017

MASCALLS

Mascalls School

COURT ROAD

6

Mile Oak

Mascalls Pound Farm

MAIDSTONE ROAD

B2160

CHANTLERS

HILL

WATERMANS LA

WATERMA...

Brick Kiln Wood

E
F
G
H

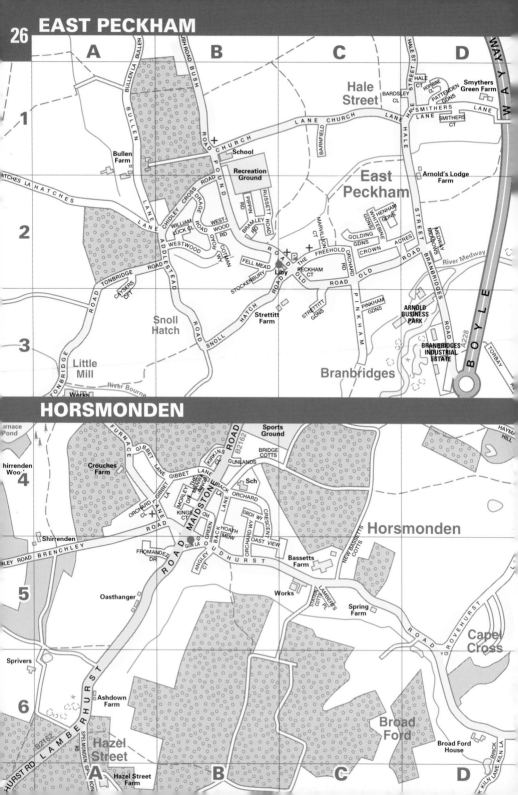

EAST PECKHAM

A B C D WAY

1

Hale Street

BULLEN LA
BULLEN
USH ROAD
BUSH
BULLEN
BULLEN LA
LANE CHURCH
LANE
HALE STREET
HALE STREET
HALE
HOPINE CL
BARDSLEY CL
SMITHERS CL
PATTENDEN GDNS
SMITHERS CT
Smythers Green Farm
SMITHERS LANE

Bullen Farm
CHURCH
School
Recreation Ground
BARNFIELD ROAD
HALE

ATCHES LA HATCHES LA
HATCHES LA

East Peckham

Arnold's Lodge Farm

2

ROAD
POUND
ROAD
LANE
CHIDLEY CROSS ROAD
ADDLESTEAD ROAD
DRAGE ROAD
WILLIAM LUCK CL
WEST WOOD RD
WESTWOOD
COTMAN WY
BRAMLEY ROAD
RUSSETT ROAD
PIPPIN RD
FELL MEAD
STOCKENBURY
ROAD
Liby
PECKHAM CT
THE OLD
MARVILLON CT
FREEHOLD RD
ORCHARD RD
OLD ROAD
HENHAM GDNS
WHITEBINE
GOLDING GDNS
CROWN
ACRES
STREET
MEDWAY MEADOWS
River Medway
BRANBRIDGES

TONBRIDGE ROAD
CAYSERS CT
ROAD
SNOLL
HATCH
ROAD
Strettitt Farm
STRETTITT GDNS
PINKHAM
PINKHAM GDNS
ARNOLD BUSINESS PARK
BRANBRIDGES ROAD

Snoll Hatch

3

TONBRIDGE ROAD

Little Mill

SNOLL ROAD

BRANBRIDGES INDUSTRIAL ESTATE
A228
TORBAY
BOYLE

River Bourne
Works
Branbridges

HORSMONDEN

A B C D

urnace Pond

hirrenden Woo'

4

FURNACE LANE
GIBBET LANE
GIBBET LANE
GIBBET LANE
KIRKINS
B2162
ROAD
Sports Ground
BRIDGE COTTS
GUNLANDS
Sch
HAYMA
HILL

Crouches Farm

ORCHARD CL
MORLEY DR
THE MWS
KINGS CT
MAIDSTONE ROAD
BACK LANE
BACK ORCHARD LA
HOATH MDW
ORCHARD WY
CRESCENT
ORCH WY
OAST VIEW
Horsmonden

Shirrenden

BRENCHLEY
CHLEY ROAD
BRENCHLEY

FROMANDEZ DR
GUN LA
ANGLEY CT
GREEN
UDHURST
Bassetts Farm
NEW BASSETTS COTTS

5

Oasthanger

Works
LAMBERTS PL
STATION COTTS
Spring Farm
ROAD
GROVEHURST
Capel Cross

Sprivers

6

LAMBERHURST
SPELMONDEN RD
Ashdown Farm

B2162
HURST RD

Hazel Street

A
Hazel Street Farm
B C
Broad Ford
Broad Ford House
KILN LANE
KILN LANE
BRICK
KILN LA
D

A B C D

1

2

3

4

5

6

GOUDHURST ROAD

Dogkennel Farm

Hotel

Whitewell Oasts

The Breach Farm

Wilsley Pound

A229

A262

GOUDHURST RD GOUD

WHITEWELL

ROAD

ANGLEY ROAD

Gravel Pit Wood

Angley Lake

Wilsley Farm

Cricket Ground

Wilsley Green

Great Swifts Manor

Burnt Bank Wood

QUAKER LANE

ANGLEY WALK

QUAKER LN

SWIFTS LN

WILLSLEY CDNS

WATERLOO

The Park

WINDMILL COTTS

Stud

Rugby Ground

Angley House

Sports Centre

Angley School

School

VICTORIA COTTS

CHURCH COTTS

OATFIELD CL

OATFIELD WAY

CARRIERS

Recreation Ground

WATERLOO ROAD

Cranbrook

Angley Wood

SHEAFE DRIVE

WHEATFIELD

WHEATFIELD CL

LEA

HENDLEY DR

PROPE WALK

JEMPSONS

DRIVE

RECTORY FIELDS

Liby

JOCKEY LA

Mus

BARHAM DR

Sewage Works

ANGLEY RD

WHEATFIELD DRIVE

JOYCE CLOSE

CROWN CT

CAUSTON RD

BANK ST

RECTORY ROAD

STONE ST

STREET

THE TANYARD

Theatre School

Baker's Cross

Goddards Green

NEW ROAD

HIGH

Police Sta

Council Offices

Fire Sta

Superstore

CRANE LANE

IMBER CT

THE CREST

THE HILL

TARBUTT

DUNSELLS

ST DUNSTANS

BRK SIDE

LION ST

BRAMLEY

HIPPOS

OR HOPES

BROOK

CKENDEN

FRYTHE CL

Amb Sta

HAMMELL MWS

BAKERS CROSS WAY

RUSSELLS YD

GOLFORD ROAD

GOLFORD

Paddo Farm

Goddards Green Farm

GREENWAY

GODDARDS CL

ORCHARD WY

HARTLEY ROAD ANGLEY

HIGH STREET

Brick Kiln Farm

Crane Brook

FREIGHT LANE

FRYTHE WK

BROADCLOTH

NORMAN

MIDDLE GARTH

FRYTHE WAY

TURNER WAY

WINCH

PENNY FIELDS

A AVENUE

KIRBY

DOROTHY

CRIES

PEAR TREE

APSER

TOWN MDW

FRYTHE

AVENUE

TILSDEN WAY

TILSDEN LANE

Hancock's Farm

A229

Turnden

Mount Ephraim

Tilsden

Tils Farm

A B C D

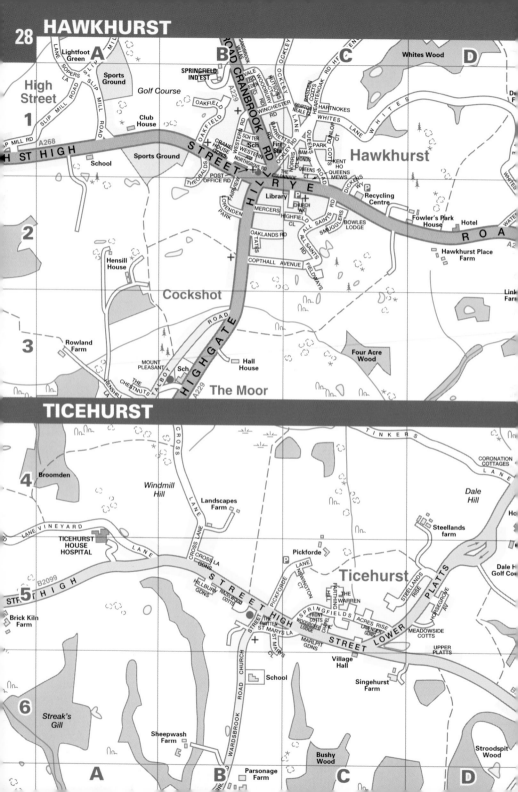

A B C D

1

Scamperdale

Gaywood Farm

HOMESTEAD RD

FAIRMEAD RD

Swan Lane Farm

B2026 ROAD MAIN

OAKFIELD RD

HILDERS CL

HILL-CREST RD

HIGHFIELDS ROAD

BROWN FIELDS

Marlpit Hill

LYNMEAD CL

ELM COTTS

ASHCOMBE DR

Marlhurst

MEADOW LANE

SWAN LANE

SWAN

PIT

MARLPIT

LANE

LANE RIDGE WY

SWAN RIDGE WY

SWAN RIDGE

Mowshurst B2027

FOUR ELMS RD

2

EL REL

Football Ground

ROAD

DERS

LANE

HILDERS

P ALBION

SUNNYSIDE

EDENBRIDGE

Breezehurst Farm

Hamsell Mead Farm

ST BRELADES CT
Caravan Park

ENTERPRISE

WAY STATION

FIRCROFT WAY

GREAT MEAD

INDUSTRIAL ESTATE

INDUSTRIAL ESTATE

COMMERCE WY

FIRCROFT WAY

MALLARD WY

HERON CL

WOODLAND GRO

KESTREL DR

SPEEDWELL CL

BRIAR CL

WAYSIDE DR

FOXGLOVE CLOVER

WAINDHOUSE

PLOVER CL

FARMSTEAD

HARROW WAY

OXFIELD

STACKFIELD

ROWFIELD

STONEYFIELD

SMITHYFIELD

1 WOODPECKER CL
2 SORRELL CL
3 BROOK CT
4 TEMPLARS CT

Sewage Works

3

SKINNERS

Spitals Cross

GRESHAMS WAY

GOODWIN

CROUCH HO COTTS

HOLLY COTTS

PLOUGH

FARMSTEAD

DR

HOPGARDEN CL

FOUR

ELMS

ROAD

Driving Range

nbridge Golf ountry Club

ROUCH

HOUSE

DRIVE

ORCHARD

CEDAR

STANBRIDGE RD

PINE GRO

PARK VIEW CL

WESTWAYS

Eden Valley School

LANE

Skinners Farm

4

Crouch House Farm

Crouch House Green

CROUCH

HOUSE

ROAD

CHESTNUT GRO

STANGROVE

HAW-THORN CL

PARK

MOLES MEAD

WELLINGTONIA WY

SCHOOL FIELD

PENLEE CL

Edenbridge Leisure Centre & Swimming Pool

i

Hall

EDENBRIDGE TOWN

Edenbridge

5

Skeynes Park

SPRINGFIELD ROAD

SPRING-LINES

MANOR HO GDNS

MANOR ROAD

ASH CL

MANOR HO GDNS

STANGROVE ROAD

HATLAND

BARN HAWE

LINGFIELD ROAD

Clinic

STATION APPROACH

GORDON HENRY HO

GRANGE

FLOWERS CL

CROFT LA

FORGE

FRONT FLD

CROFT CT

READLEY CLOSE

GREENFIELD

Sch

QUEENS

CHURCH FIELD

Cemy

CROFT

STREATHER

THE PLAT

STREET

Liby

CP

HIGH

ROAD

THE LIMES

TANNERS MEAD

COOMBE

Council Offices

Mus

Market Mkt

S/store

LEATHER

DOGGETS

PENNS

LUCILINA DR

AVIGNAN WY

COBBETS WY

LEATHER

THE SQ

CHURCH ST

RIVERSIDE

CHURCH STREET

RIVERSIDE CT

River Eden

6

FLDRD

ROAD

SKEENES

Recreation Ground

Mill Race

Fire Sta

KATHERINE RD

VICTORIA RD

VICTORIA CL

MILL HILL COTTS

MILL STREET

WATERLAKES

ASHBYS RD

MONT

C

HEVER

ROAD

EDENBRIDGE TRADING CENTRE

WARSOP IND EST

ROAD HEVER

Kent Brook

B2026

HOSPITAL

HILL MILL

A B C D

MEAD RD

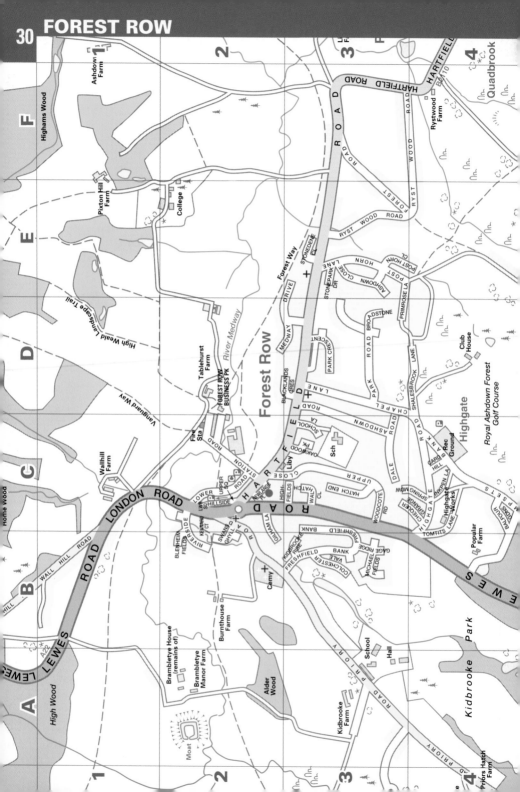

Forest Row

Highams Wood

Ashdown Farm

Pixton Hill Farm

College

High Weald Landscape Trail

Tablehurst Farm

FOREST ROW BUSINESS PK

River Medway

Vanguard Way

Wallhill Farm

Fire Sta

Home Wood

High Wood

WALL HILL ROAD

LEWES ROAD

LONDON ROAD

BLENHEIM RISE

RIVERSIDE

KENWARD CT

SWANS CT

SHILLSIDE

LWR SQ

UPPER SQ

LOWER SQ

STATION ROAD

HARTFIELD ROAD

BRAMBLETYE PL

CHILHAM LA

Brambletye House (remains of)

Brambletye Manor Farm

Burnthouse Farm

Moat

Alder Wood

Cemy

Forest Way

STONEDENE CL

MEDWAY DRIVE

BLACKLANDS CRES

FIELD LANE

SCHOOL LA

OAKWOOD Pk

Liby

Sch

FIELDS

WALL HATCH

HATCH END

PARK CRESC

BROADSTONE

ROAD BRO

PARK

ROAD

UPPER

DALE ROAD

ASHDOWN ROAD

WOODCOTE RD

CHECKER GRANGE

SPRING MDW

HIGHGATE HILL

LINDEN LA

Highgate Lane Works

CHAPEL LANE

SHALESBROOK LANE

ASHDOWN CLOSE

STONEPARK CLOSE

HORN

POST HORN CL

PRIMROSE LA

POST

Club House

Highgate

Rec Ground

P

Royal Ashdown Forest Golf Course

HARTFIELD ROAD

FOREST RYST

RYST WOOD ROAD

RYST WOOD

B2110

Rystwood Farm

Quadbrook

KIDBROOKE FIELDS

FRESHFIELD BANK

GAGE RIDGE

VALE

BANK

MICHAEL FIELDS

COLCHESTER

FRESHFIELD

TOMTITS LANE

Popular Farm

BALTHOUR LIONS RD

MPSETS

School

Hall

PRIORY ROAD

Kidbrooke Farm

PRIORY

Kidbrooke Park

Priors Hatch Farm

LEWES

The Index includes some names for which there is insufficient space on the maps. These names are indicated by an * and are followed by the nearest adjoining thoroughfare.

Acer Av TN2 17 F6
Acorn Cl TN12 24 C3
Acres Rise TN5 28 C5
Adam Cl TN6 22 C3
Adam Ct TN10 6 C5
Addlestead Rd TN12 26 B2
Alamein Cl TN6 21 E6
Albany TN9 9 G5
Albany Hill TN2 15 E6
Albert Rd TN9 9 E4
Albert St TN1 3 D1
Albion Cl TN11 7 E3
Albion Rd TN1 15 E6
Albion Way TN8 29 B2
Alder Cl TN4 15 F2
Alderbrook Cl TN6 22 B3
Alderbrook Cotts TN6 22 B3
Alderbrook Path TN6 22 B3
Alderbrook Way TN6 22 B3
Alders Cotts TN12 24 A5
Alders Mdw TN9 8 C2
Alders Rd TN12 24 A4
Aldervale Cotts TN6 22 B2
Aldwych TN10 6 A3
Aldwych Cl TN10 6 A3
Alexander Ct TN1 3 B2
Alexandra Rd,
Mayfield TN20 23 D4
Alexandra Rd,
Tonbridge TN9 9 E4
Alexandra Ter TN20 23 D4
Alice Bright La TN6 22 A2
All Saints Rd,
Cranbrook TN18 28 C2
All Saints Rd,
Tunbridge Wells TN4 14 D5
All Saints Rise TN4 14 D5
Allan Cl TN4 13 F5
Allandale Rd TN2 15 F5
Alliance Way TN12 25 F3
Allington Dr TN10 6 C5
Allington Rd TN12 25 F3
Amberleaze Dr TN2 18 D3
Amberley Cl TN9 8 D4
Amherst Rd TN4 14 C6
Amhurst Bank Rd TN2 24 A5
Andrew Rd TN4 15 E3
Andrews Cl TN2 15 F6
Angel Centre TN9 9 F3
Angel La TN9 9 E3
Angel Walk TN9 9 E3
Angley Cl TN6 26 B5
Angley Rd TN17 27 A5
Angley Walk TN17 27 C3
Apple Cl TN12 25 F4
Apple Tree La TN2 15 F3
Appletons TN11 7 E3
Apsley St TN4 13 F5
Argyle Rd TN4 14 D1
Arne Cl TN10 6 B4
Arnold Bsns Pk TN12 26 D3
Arundel Cl TN9 8 D4
Arundel Rd TN1 3 B5
Ash Cl, Edenbridge TN8 29 B5
Ash Cl,
Tunbridge Wells TN2 17 F6
Ash Ct TN2 16 C1
Ashburnham Rd TN6 9 F1
Ashbys Cl TN8 29 C6
Ashbys Yd TN9 9 F3
Ashcombe Dr TN8 29 B2
Ashcroft Rd TN12 25 G5
Ashden Walk TN10 5 H3
Ashdown Cl,
Forest Row RH18 30 E3
Ashdown Cl,
Tunbridge Wells TN4 16 B1
Ashdown Ct TN6 20 C4
Ashdown Rd RH18 30 C3
Ashenden Walk TN2 15 G3
Asher Reeds TN3 13 D5
Ashes La TN11 6 B1
Ashlands TN6 21 F5
Ashleigh Gdns TN6 20 C2

Ashley Gdns,
Mayfield TN20 23 B5
Ashley Gdns,
Tunbridge Wells TN4 13 E5
Ashley Park Rd TN4 13 E5
Ashley Pk TN4 13 E5
Ashley Rd TN11 4 D5
Aspen Way TN4 15 F2
Auckland Rd TN1 15 E5
Audley Av TN9 8 C3
Audley Rise TN9 8 C3
Aultmore Ct TN2 17 F2
Avenue Du Puy TN9 9 F3
Avebury Av TN9 9 E3
Aviemore Rd TN6 20 B4
Avon Cl TN10 5 H5
Avon St TN1 15 E6

Back La TN12 26 B4
Badgers Cl TN6 20 C3
Badgers Holt TN2 15 G6
Badsell Rd TN12 24 C3
Bakers Cross TN17 27 C5
Balaclava La TN5 19 E1
Baldock Rd TN5 19 D3
Balfour Gdns RH18 30 C4
Ballard Way TN12 25 H3
Balliol Cotts TN5 19 F4
Baltic Rd TN9 9 H5
Bank St, Cranbrook TN17 27 B4
Bank St, Tonbridge TN9 9 F2
Bankside TN5 19 D2
Banner Farm Rd TN2 3 D6
Barchester Way TN10 6 C4
Barclay Av TN10 6 C6
Barden Park Rd TN9 8 D3
Barden Rd, Tonbridge TN9 8 D3
Barden Rd,
Tunbridge Wells TN3 10 A5
Bardsley Cl TN12 26 C1
Barham Dr TN17 27 C4
Barn Hawe TN8 29 C5
Barnetts Cl TN4 15 E3
Barnetts Rd TN1 10 B2
Barnetts Way TN4 15 E3
Barnfield,
Crowborough TN6 21 E4
Barnfield,
Tonbridge TN12 26 C1
Barnfield,
Tunbridge Wells TN2 16 C6
Barons Ct TN4 14 D6
Barretts Rd TN18 28 B1
Barrow La TN3 13 C7
Bassetts Rd TN18 28 C1
Bassetts Forge TN5 19 D3
Batchelors TN2 18 E2
Bayhall Rd TN2 17 E2
Bayham Ct TN5 19 D2
Bayham Rd TN2 16 C5
Beacon Cl TN6 20 C4
Beacon Gdns TN6 20 C3
Beacon Rd TN6 20 A6
Beacon Rd West TN6 20 B4
Beaglees Wood Rd TN2 18 E2
Beaulieu Rd TN10 5 G6
Beaumont Ct TN2 16 C4
Beaver Cl TN6 21 E5
Bedford Rd TN4 14 C2
Bedford Ter TN1 3 B5
Beech Ct TN2 17 F1
Beech Hurst TN2 18 D3
Beech Manor TN2 17 F3
Beech St TN1 3 D1
Beecham Rd TN10 6 B4
Beeches Farm Rd TN6 21 E5
Beeches Rd TN6 21 E5
Beechmont Rise TN10 5 G2
Belfield Rd TN2 18 D4
Belgrave Rd TN1 3 C1
Belgrove TN1 3 C5
Beltring Rd TN12 14 C5
Belvedere Gdns TN6 21 E6
Benhall Mill Rd TN2,3 17 E5
Bentham Hill TN3 14 A2
Bentley Path TN6 22 E2
Berkeley Cl TN2 18 E3
Berkeley Pl*,
Berkeley Rd TN1 3 C5
Berkeley Rd TN1 3 B6
Beulah Rd TN1 17 E1

Beverley Cres TN9 8 C5
Bickmore Way TN9 9 F1
Bidborough Ridge TN3,4 11 E4
Birch Cl, Tonbridge TN11 4 D6
Birch Cl,
Tunbridge Wells TN2 15 F5
Birch Rd TN12 25 G4
Birch Way TN2 15 F4
Birchden Cotts TN3 23 D3
Birchden Rd TN3 23 D3
Birches Cl TN6 20 D2
Birchetts Av TN3 13 B6
Birchwood Av TN4 11 F5
Bird La TN5 19 A3
Birdcage Walk TN1 3 C5
Birken Rd TN2 16 D5
Birling Dr TN2 16 D5
Birling Park Av TN2 16 D5
Birling Rd TN2 16 D5
Bishops Cl TN4 16 B2
Bishops Down Park Rd
TN4 16 B1
Bishops Down Rd TN4 16 B2
Bishops Mews TN9 9 F4
Bishops Oak Ride TN10 5 G4
Blackberry Way TN12 25 H4
Blackhurst La TN2 15 H6
Blacklands Cres RH18 30 D3
Blackmans La TN11 7 C3
Blackness Rd TN6 20 D5
Blacksmiths La TN5 19 F2
Blackthorn Av TN5 15 E3
Blake Ct*, Brook Rd TN2 15 F4
Blakeway TN2 15 F4
Blatchington Rd TN2 16 D4
Blenheim Flds RH18 30 B2
Bliss Way TN10 6 C5
Bocking Cl TN5 19 D3
Bondfield Cl TN4 14 D2
Booker Cl TN6 21 E5
Bordyke TN9 9 F2
Botany TN9 9 F3
Botany Ind Est TN9 9 F3
Boundary Rd TN2 17 F4
Bounds Oak Way TN4 11 F4
Bourne Cl TN9 9 G1
Bourne Grange La TN1 7 C3
Bourne La TN9 9 F1
Bowen Rd TN4 13 E5
Bowles Lodge TN18 28 C2
Bowls Pl TN2 25 G3
Boyle Way TN12 26 D3
Boyne Pk TN4 3 A2
Bracken Cl,
Crowborough TN6 21 G5
Bracken Cl,
Tunbridge Wells TN2 15 G6
Bracken Rd TN2 15 G6
Bracken Walk TN10 5 G4
Bradford St TN9 9 E3
Bramble Cft TN6 21 E4
Bramble Cl TN11 5 E6
Bramble Walk TN2 15 F4
Bramley Dr TN17 27 C5
Bramley Gdns TN12 25 F3
Bramley Rd TN12 26 B2

**Branbridges
Ind Est TN12 26 D3**
Branbridges Rd TN12 26 D1
Brantingham Cl TN9 8 C5
Breedon Av TN4 14 C2
Brenchley Rd TN12 26 A5
Brendon Cl TN2 15 F6
Bretland Rd TN4 13 F5
Brewers Gro TN20 23 B5
Brian Cres TN4 14 D3
Brian Ct TN9 9 E2
Briar Cl TN8 29 C3
Briar Walk TN10 5 H4
Brick Kiln La TN12 26 D6
Brickenden Rd TN17 27 C5
Brickfields TN2 18 E2
Brickmead TN6 21 E5
Brickworks Cl TN9 8 D6
Bridge Bsns Pk TN12 24 C2
Bridge Cl TN9 9 F4
Bridge Cotts TN4 26 B4
Bridge Ct TN4 16 B4
Bridger Way TN6 20 D5
Bright Ridge TN6 14 B3
Brincliffe TN6 20 C3

Brindles Fld TN9 8 D5
Brionne Gdns TN9 9 G4
Britten Cl TN6 6 B4
Broad Gro TN2 16 C5
Broad Oak TN3 23 C2
Broad Oak Cl TN2 16 C5
Broadcloth TN17 27 C6
Broadcroft TN2 16 C5
Broadmead TN2 16 B5
Broadmead Av TN2 16 B5
Broadstone RH18 30 D3
Broadwater Down TN2 16 A5
Broadwater La TN2 16 B4
Broadwater Rise TN2 16 C4
Broadway TN6 20 D3
Broadway*, High St TN11 7 D3
Brokes Way TN9 15 E3
Brook Cl TN6 21 G5
Brook Ct TN8 29 C3
Brook La TN9 9 G2
Brook Rd TN2 15 F4
Brook St TN9 8 C4
Brook Ter TN6 20 B2
Brook Vw TN6 20 B2
Brookfield Ct TN4 14 C2
Brookfields TN11 7 D2
Brookhurst Gdns TN4 11 F5
Brooklands TN2 15 F5
Brooklands Av TN6 22 B2
Brookmead TN11 4 D5
Brooks Cl TN10 6 A3
Brookside TN17 27 C5
Broom La TN3 13 B6
Broom Pk TN3 13 B7
Broomhill Park Rd TN4 14 B3
Broomhill Rd TN3 12 F4
Broomwaters TN11 7 C1
Brownings TN8 29 B2
Brungers Walk TN10 5 G6
Brunswick Ter TN1 3 B6
Bryants Flds TN6 20 C3
Buckingham Rd TN1 3 C5
Bucklers Cl TN2 17 E2
Bullen La TN12 26 A1
Buller Cl TN6 21 E5
Bullfinch Cl TN12 25 G5
Bullingstone Cotts TN3 12 B2
Bullingstone La TN3 12 B2
Bullion Cl TN12 25 F4
Bulls Pl TN2 18 D3
Burdett Rd,
Crowborough TN6 21 G5
Burdett Rd,
Tunbridge Wells TN4 13 E5
Burns Cres TN9 8 D5
Burnt House La TN3 12 C4
Burnt Oak Rd TN6 22 B4
Burrswood Villas TN3 23 C1
Burslem Rd TN2 15 G5
Bush Rd TN12 26 B1
Bushy Gill TN3 13 C6
Butler Cl TN6 20 C5
Buttercup Cl TN12 25 G5
Byng Rd TN4 16 B1
Byrneside TN11 4 D6

Cabbage Stalk La TN4 16 A4
Cadogan Gdns TN1 3 C3
Cage Green Rd TN10 5 H5
Caistor Rd TN1 8 D3
Caley Rd TN2 15 F4
Calverley Ct TN1 17 E2
Calverley Park Cres TN1 3 D3
Calverley Park Gdns TN1 3 D3
Calverley Pk TN1 3 D3
Calverley Rd TN1 3 C2
Calverley St TN1 3 D2
Cambrian Rd TN4 15 E4
Cambridge Gdns TN1 3 D5
Cambridge St TN2 17 E2
Cambridge Villas TN1 3 B3
Camden Av TN2 18 C4
Camden Cl,
Pembury TN2 18 D4
Camden Ct,
Tunbridge Wells TN1 3 D1
Camden Hill TN2 3 D5
Camden Pk TN2 17 E3
Camden Rd TN1 3 C2
Campbell Rd TN4 14 C5

**Cannon Bri Works
TN9** 9 G2
Cannon La TN9 9 G2
Canterbury Cres TN10 6 A5
Canterbury Rd TN2 18 E4
Card Hill RH18 30 C4
Cardinal Cl TN9 9 G5
Carlton Cl TN10 6 A3
Carlton Cres TN1 17 E2
Carlton Rd TN1 17 E2
Carpenters La TN11 7 C1
Carriers Rd TN17 27 C4
Carville Av TN4 14 C2
Castle Flds TN9 9 E2
Castle Rd TN4 3 A3
Castle St,
Southborough TN4 14 C1
Castle St, Tonbridge TN9 9 E2
Castle St,
Tunbridge Wells TN1 3 B5
Castle Ter TN11 7 D3
Castle Walk TN5 19 D3
Catherine Pl TN1 3 D3
Causton Rd TN1 27 B4
Cavalry Cl TN10 6 A3
Cavendish Cl TN10 6 A3
Cavendish Ct TN9 9 G2
Cavendish Dr TN2 3 D6
Caxton La TN11 7 D3
Caysers Cft TN12 26 A3
Cedar Cres TN10 5 H3
Cedar Ct TN4 14 C6
Cedar Dr TN8 29 B4
Cedar Lodge TN4 16 B2
Cedar Ridge TN2 15 F6
Cemetery La TN11 7 E2
Chaffinch Way TN12 25 G5
Chalket La TN2 18 C4
Challenger Cl TN12 25 F4
Chancellor Ho TN4 16 B2
Chandos Rd TN1 15 E6
Chantlers Hill TN12 25 G6
Chapel Grn TN6 20 D4
Chapel La RH18 30 D3
Chapel Pl,
Tunbridge Wells TN1 3 B6
Chapel Pl,
Wadhurst TN5 28 C5
Chapman Way TN2 15 E3
Charity Farm Way TN6 21 E3
Charles Ct TN2 17 F2
Charles St TN4 14 C3
Charlottes Cotts TN11 10 A2
Charlton Ter TN9 9 F2
Charltons Way TN4 16 A4
Chaucer Gdns TN9 8 C5
Chenies Cl TN2 16 C6
Chequer Grange RH18 30 C4
Chequers Cl TN6 21 E4
Chequers Way TN6 21 E4
Cherry Gardens Hill TN3 23 A3
Cherry Gro TN10 6 B5
Cherry Tree Rd,
Tonbridge TN10 6 A3
Cherry Tree Rd,
Tunbridge Wells TN2 16 B4
Cherwell Cl TN10 5 G6
Chesfield Cl TN11 7 E2
Chester Av TN2 17 F3
Chestnut Av TN4 14 C5
Chestnut Cl,
Edenbridge TN8 29 B4
Chestnut Cl,
Tunbridge Wells TN4 14 D3
Chestnut Ct TN2 16 C5
Chestnut Walk TN9 8 C2
Cheviot Cl TN9 5 H6
Chichester Rd TN9 8 C5
Chidley Cross Rd TN12 26 B2
Chieveley Dr TN2 17 F5
Chilston Cl TN4 14 D6
Chilston Rd TN4 14 D6
Chiltern Walk TN2 17 F1
Chiltern Way TN9 9 F1
Chilternhurst TN8 29 A3
Christchurch Av TN1 3 C5
Church Cotts TN17 27 B4
Church Rd TN8 29 C5
Church Rd TN11 10 B2
Church La,
East Peckham TN12 26 B1

Grange Cl, Crowborough TN6 20 B5
Grange Cl, Edenbridge TN8 29 C4
Grange Gdns TN4 13 F5
Grange Rd TN4 13 F5
Grantley Cl TN1 3 B5
Granville Rd TN1 15 E6
Graycoats Dr TN6 20 D4
Great Bounds Dr TN4 11 F4
Great Brooms Rd TN4 15 E3
Great Courtlands TN3 13 C5
Great Elms TN11 7 D2
Great Footway TN3 13 C6
Great Hall Arc TN1 3 C4
Great Lodge Retail Pk TN2 15 G2
Great Mead TN8 29 B3
Grecian Rd TN1 3 C5
Green La, Crowborough TN6 21 F4
Green La, Tonbridge TN12 25 G5
Green Rd TN12 26 B5
Green Sq TN5 19 E3
Green View Av TN11 10 B2
Green Way TN2 15 G3
Greenfield TN8 29 C4
Greenfield Cl TN4 12 E4
Greenfrith Dr TN10 5 G3
Greenleas TN2 18 C3
Greentrees Av TN10 6 B5
Greenview Cres TN11 4 D6
Greenway TN17 27 A5
Greggs Wood Rd TN2 15 G4
Gresham Cl TN10 6 A3
Greshams Way TN8 29 A4
Gromenfield TN3 23 C2
Groombridge Hill TN3 23 C1
Grosvenor Bri TN1 15 E6
Grosvenor Pk TN1 3 B1
Grosvenor Rd TN1 3 B1
Grosvenor Walk TN1 3 C1
Grove Av TN1 3 C5
Grove Hill Cl TN1 3 C4
Grove Hill Gdns TN1 3 D5
Grove Hill Rd TN1 3 C4
Grovehurst La TN12 26 D6
Grover St TN1 3 D2
Guardian Bsns Pk TN2 15 H1
Guards Cl TN10 6 A3
Guestwick TN10 6 C5
Guildford Rd TN1 3 C5
Gun La TN12 26 B5
Gunlands TN12 26 B4

Hadley Ct TN4 14 C5
Hadlow Down Rd TN6 22 C4
Hadlow Pk TN11 7 E2
Hadlow Rd, Higham Wood TN10 6 C6
Hadlow Rd, Tonbridge TN9 9 F2
Hadlow Stair Rd TN10 6 C6
Hailstone Cl TN11 7 D3
Hale Ct TN12 26 D1
Hale St TN12 26 D1
Half Moon La TN11 4 C4
Halland Ct TN8 29 B5
Halls Cotts TN5 19 E2
Halls Hole Rd TN2 17 F3
Hamble Rd TN10 5 G5
Hamilton Ct TN4 14 D6
Hamilton Ho*, Hamilton Ct TN4 14 D6
Hammonds TN18 28 C1
Handel Walk TN10 6 B5
Hanover Rd TN1 3 B2
Harding Av TN4 11 E5
Hardwick Rd TN11 4 D4
Harecombe Rd TN6 20 C6
Harecombe Rise TN6 20 D6
Harescroft TN2 16 C6
Hargate Cl TN2 16 B6
Harland Way TN4 11 F4
Harlequin La TN6 20 C5
Harlequin Pl TN6 20 C6
Harmer Ct TN4 14 C2
Harmony St TN4 16 A1
Harries Rd TN2 15 F4
Harrow Cl TN8 29 C3
Hartfield Cl TN10 6 B5
Hartfield Rd RH18 30 C2
Hartley Rd TN17 27 A6
Hartnokes TN18 28 C1
Harvest Rd TN10 5 H4
Hasletts Cl TN1 15 E6
Hastings Rd TN2 18 D4
Hatch End RH18 30 C3
Hatches La TN12 26 A2
Havelock Rd TN9 9 E2
Havering Cl TN2 15 H5
Hawden Cl TN11 5 E6
Hawden La TN11 8 C1
Hawden Rd TN9 9 E2
Hawkenbury Cl TN2 17 F4
Hawkenbury Mead TN2 17 F4
Hawkenbury Rd TN2 17 F4
Hawthorn Cl TN8 29 B4
Hawthorn Walk, Tonbridge TN10 5 H3
Hawthorn Walk, Tunbridge Wells TN2 15 G3
Haydens Mws TN9 9 F1
Hayesden La TN11 10 B4
Haymans Hill TN12 26 D4
Haywain Cl TN12 25 G5
Hazel Shaw TN10 5 H4
Hazelbank TN3 13 C6
Hazelwood Cl TN2 15 G3
Hazelwood Cotts TN5 28 B5
Headley Ct TN8 29 C4
Headway Ct TN4 13 E5
Heartenoak Rd TN18 28 C1
Heather Bank TN12 25 H4
Heather Walk, Crowborough TN6 21 G5
Heather Walk, Tonbridge TN10 5 G3
Heathfields TN2 17 F1
Heathview TN4 14 B1
Heavegate Rd TN6 20 A5
Hectorage Rd TN9 9 F4
Helen Keller Cl TN10 5 H6
Hendley Dr TN17 27 B4
Henham Gdns TN12 26 C2
Henley Cl TN2 17 F1
Henley Rd TN12 25 G3
Henshill La TN18 28 A3
Henwood Green Rd TN2 18 E2
Henwoods Cres TN2 18 E4
Henwoods Mt TN2 18 E4
Hermitage Ct TN9 9 F2
Herne Down TN6 22 B2
Herne Rd TN6 20 D6
Heron Cl TN8 29 C3
Herons Way TN2 18 E2
Heskett Pk TN2 18 E3
Hever Rd TN8 29 C6
High Beeches TN2 15 F5
High Broom La TN6 22 A3
High Broom Rd TN6 22 A2
High Brooms Ind Est TN2 15 F3
High Brooms Rd TN4 15 E3
High Cross Flds TN6 20 D3
High Hilden Cl TN10 5 F6
High House La TN11 6 D2
High Rocks La TN3 13 E8
High St, Bidborough TN3 10 D4
High St, Cranbrook TN17 27 A5
High St, Crowborough TN6 20 D3
High St, Edenbridge TN8 29 C5
High St, Hadlow TN11 7 D3
High St, Hawkhurst TN18 28 A1
High St, Leigh TN11 10 A2
High St, Mayfield TN20 23 B5
High St, Pembury TN2 18 B3
High St, Ticehurst TN5 28 A5
High St, Tonbridge TN9 9 E4
High St, Tunbridge Wells TN1 3 B5
High St, Wadhurst TN5 19 E3
High Woods La TN2 17 F3
Higham Gdns TN10 6 C5
Higham La TN11 6 B1
Higham School Rd TN10 6 B4
Highfield Cl, Cranbrook TN18 28 B2
Highfield Cl, Tunbridge Wells TN2 18 D3
Highfield Rd TN4 15 E4
Highfields RH18 30 C2
Highfields Rd TN8 29 B1
Highgate Hill TN18 28 B3
Highgate Rd RH18 30 C4
Highgrove TN2 16 D5
Highlands Cl TN6 20 C3
Highlands Ho*, Calverley Rd TN2 17 E2
Hilbert Cl TN2 15 E6
Hilbert Rd TN2 15 E5
Hilden Av TN11 5 E6
Hilden Park Rd TN11 5 E6
Hildenborough Rd TN11 10 B1
Hildenfields TN6 8 D1
Hilders Cl TN8 29 B1
Hilders Farm Cl TN6 21 F5
Hilders Farm Ct TN6 21 F5
Hilders La TN8 29 A2
Hill Cl TN6 20 C5
Hill Crest TN4 14 D3
Hill St TN1 3 C1
Hill Top TN9 9 E5
Hill View Rd, Tonbridge TN11 5 E5
Hill View Rd, Tunbridge Wells TN4 13 E5
Hillbury Gdns TN5 28 B5
Hillcrest Dr TN2 15 F4
Hillcrest Rd TN8 29 B1
Hillgarth TN4 14 D4
Hillrise TN6 21 F4
Hillside, Forest Row RH18 30 C2
Hillside, Tonbridge TN9 8 D5
Hither Chantlers TN3 13 D6
Hoadleys La TN6 20 B1
Hoath Mdw TN12 26 B4
Holden Cnr TN4 14 B2
Holden Park Rd TN4 14 C3
Holden Rd TN4 14 B2
Holford St TN9 9 E3
Hollin Cl TN4 16 B1
Hollow Trees Dr TN11 10 C2
Holly Cotts TN8 29 A4
Holly Ct TN6 20 B4
Hollydene Rd TN5 19 E1
Hollyshaw Cl TN2 17 E3
Holmewood Rd TN4 15 E4
Holmewood Ridge TN3 13 B6
Holmhurst Cl TN4 16 B2
Holmsdale Cl TN5 19 D2
Home Farm La TN2 15 G3
Homestead Rd TN8 29 B1
Homewood Rd TN3 13 B6
Hookswood Cl TN6 21 E3
Hop Bine Cl TN12 26 D1
Hop Pocket La TN12 25 G2
Hope Av TN11 7 C2
Hope Ter TN4 14 C6
Hopgarden Cl TN8 29 C3
Hopgarden Rd TN10 6 A5
Hopwood Gdns TN4 14 D5
Horizon Cl TN4 15 E3
Hornbeam Av TN4 15 F2
Hornbeam Cl TN12 25 F5
Horns Lodge La TN11 5 E2
Horsegrove Av TN5 28 D5
Houselands Rd TN9 9 E2
Howard Gdns TN2 16 C4
Humboldt Ct TN2 15 F6
Hungershall Park Cl TN4 16 A4
Hungershall Pk TN4 16 A4
Hunt Rd TN10 6 B4
Hunter Seal TN11 8 B2
Hunters Way TN2 16 B4
Huntingdon Cl TN17 27 C5
Huntingdon Rd TN6 20 D6
Huntleys Pk TN4 14 B6
Hurlingham Cl TN10 6 A3
Hurstwood La TN4 16 B2
Hurstwood Pk TN4 16 B2
Hurtis Hill TN6 22 A2
Hutsons Ct TN18 28 B1
Hydehurst Cl TN6 20 D5
Hythe Cl TN4 14 C2

Imber Ct TN17 27 C5
Impala Gdns TN4 14 D5
Ingleside Dr TN6 20 C4
Inhams Wood TN6 20 B2
Inkpen La RH18 30 C4
Inner London Rd TN1 3 B3
Ironstones TN3 13 E6
Ives Rd TN9 8 C3

James Cl TN11 7 E2
Jardine Ct TN6 20 D4
Jasmine Cotts TN3 23 C1
Jeffries Way TN6 20 D2
Jempsons TN17 27 B4
Jockey La TN17 27 C4
John Spare Ct*, Whitefield Rd TN4 14 C6
John St TN4 14 C6
Jonas Dr TN5 19 D2
Jonas La TN5 19 D2
Joyce Cl TN17 27 B5
Judd Rd TN9 9 E5
Juniper Cl TN4 15 F2

Katherine Rd TN8 29 C6
Katherine Villas*, Katherine Rd TN8 29 C6
Keel Gdns TN4 14 B3
Kelvin Cl TN10 6 A3
Kemble Cl TN2 15 G4
Kemps Farm Rd TN6 21 F5
Kendal Cl TN9 9 F2
Kendal Dr TN9 9 F2
Kendal Pk TN4 14 A6
Kennard Ct RH18 30 B2
Kennet Rd TN10 5 G5
Kent Cl TN12 25 G3
Kent Ho TN18 28 C1
Kent Rd TN4 14 C5
Kentish Gdns TN2 16 B6
Kenward Ct TN11 7 D3
Kestrel Cl TN8 29 C3
Keswick Cl TN9 9 F2
Keyes Gdns TN9 8 C5
Keyworth Cl TN12 25 F3
Kibbles La TN4 14 B2
Kidbrooke Rise RH18 30 B3
Kiln La TN11 10 A2
Kiln Way TN12 25 G5
King George V Hill TN2 15 E6
King Standing Bsns Pk TN2 15 H2
King Standing Way TN2 15 H1
Kings Chase TN6 20 B3
Kings Ct, Crowborough TN6 20 C4
Kings Ct, Tonbridge TN12 26 B4
Kings Ct, Tunbridge Wells TN1 3 D3
Kings Pk TN2 17 F2
Kings Rd TN9 9 F5
Kings Toll Rd TN2 18 F3
Kingsley Ct TN5 19 F3
Kingswood Cl TN2 17 E2
Kingswood Rd TN2 17 E2
Kinnings Row TN9 9 F2
Kirby Cl TN17 27 C5
Kirby Ct TN3 13 D6
Kirkdale Rd TN1 3 D1
Kirkins Cl TN12 26 B4
Knight Rd TN10 6 A4
Knights Cl TN2 18 D2
Knights Pk TN2 15 H3
Knights Pk Leisure Complex TN2 15 H3
Knights Ridge TN2 18 D3
Knights Way TN2 15 H3
Knightsbridge Cl TN4 14 B6
Knowle Cl, Crowborough TN6 22 E2
Knowle Cl, Tunbridge Wells TN3 13 B6
Knowle Hill TN20 23 A6
Knowle Pk TN6 20 B4
Knowle Pk Rd TN20 23 A6
Knowsley Way TN11 4 C4

Laburnum Ct*, Sandhurst Rd TN2 15 F4
Ladyfern Ct*, Ferndale Cl TN2 17 F1
Ladys Gift Rd TN4 14 B3
Lake Rd TN4 16 B1
Lakeside TN2 15 G5
Lamberhurst Rd TN12 26 A6
Lambersart Cl TN4 15 F3
Lamberts Pl TN12 26 C5
Lamberts Rd TN2 15 F3
Lambourn Way TN2 17 F4
Lambs Bank TN9 9 E6
Lampington Row TN3 13 A6
Landseer Cl TN10 6 A4
Langholm Rd TN3 13 B6
Langridge Cl TN6 20 B6
Langton Rd, Langton Green TN3 13 A7
Langton Rd, Speldhurst TN3 12 C4
Langton Ridge TN3 13 D6
Lansdowne Rd, Tonbridge TN9 9 E2
Lansdowne Rd, Tunbridge Wells TN1 3 D3
Lansdowne Sq TN1 3 D2
Lanthorne Mews TN1 3 C3
Larch Cres TN10 5 H4
Larch Gro TN12 25 G4
Larkfield TN12 24 B3
Laurel Bank, Tunbridge Wells TN4 14 D4
Laurel Bank, Wadhurst TN5 19 F4
Laurel Rd TN2 15 F4
Laurel Way TN2 15 F4
Lavender Gdns TN5 28 C5
Lavender Hill TN9 9 F5
Lawn Rd TN9 9 E4
Lawrence Rd TN10 6 B4
Laxton Gdns TN12 25 F3
Le Temple Rd TN12 25 H3
Lealands Av TN11 10 B2
Lealands Cl TN3 23 C2
Leather Cl TN8 29 B6
Leathermarket TN8 29 C5
Leconfield Cl TN9 8 C5
Leggs La TN3 12 A4
Leicester Dr TN2 16 B5
Leigh Rd TN11 4 C6
Leighton Cl TN4 14 C4
Leneda Dr TN2 16 B5
Leslie Tew Ct TN10 5 G5
Lewes Rd, Forest Row RH18 30 A1
Lewes Rd, Forest Row RH18 30 B4
Lexden Lodge Ind Est TN6 21 G6
Leybank TN11 5 E6
Lime Hill Rd TN1 3 B2
Lime Tree Cl TN9 9 F2
Limekiln Ct TN6 21 F3
Lincoln Way TN6 22 B2
Linden Cl, Tonbridge TN12 25 G4
Linden Cl, Tunbridge Wells TN4 3 A6
Linden Ct TN10 5 G3
Linden Gdns TN2 16 C4
Linden Park Rd TN4 3 A6
Lingfield Rd TN8 29 A6
Link Way TN2 15 G4
Links Cl TN6 20 B5
Linnet Av TN12 25 G5
Lionel Rd TN9 8 D4
Lipscombe Rd TN2 15 F5
Liptraps La TN2 15 F4
Little Bounds TN4 11 F4
Little Footway TN3 13 C6
Little Mallett TN3 13 B6
Little Mount Sion TN1 3 B5
Little Orchards TN3 13 B6
Little Paddocks TN6 20 C5
Little Pk TN5 19 D3
Little Sunnyside TN6 20 D5
Loampits Cl TN9 9 G1
Lockington Cl TN9 8 C5
Lockside TN9 9 F2
Lodge Oak La TN9 9 G5
Lodge Rd TN9 9 E2
Lomaria Ct*, Ferndale Cl TN1 17 E1
London Rd, Crowborough TN6 20 B1
London Rd, Forest Row RH18 30 C1
London Rd, Hildenborough TN11 5 E6
London Rd, Southborough TN4 11 F4
London Rd, Tunbridge Wells TN1 3 A3
London Rd, Watts Cross TN11 4 A2
Lonewood Way TN11 7 E1
Long Mead Way TN10 5 G6
Long Meads TN3 13 D6
Long Slip TN3 13 D6
Longfield Rd TN2 15 F3
Longview Way TN2 15 F4
Lonsdale Gdns TN1 3 B4
Lordswell La TN6 20 C6
Lorenden Pk TN18 28 B2
Love La TN20 23 A5
Lovers Walk TN9 9 F1
Lower Green Rd, Pembury TN2 18 D4
Lower Green Rd, Speldhurst TN3 12 E2
Lower Grn TN11 10 A2

Lower Haysden La TN11 8 A5
Lower High St TN5 19 F3
Lower Platts TN5 28 C5
Lower Rd RH18 30 C2
Lower Saxonbury TN6 20 D4
Lower Sq RH18 30 C2
Lower St TN11 4 A5
Loxfield Cl TN20 23 A5
Loxfield Gdns TN6 21 F5
Lucilina Dr TN8 29 B6
Lucknow Rd TN12 25 G2
Lucks La TN12 25 G1
Luxford Dr TN6 21 E6
Luxford La TN6 21 E6
Luxford Rd TN6 22 C2
Lynmead Cl TN8 29 B2
Lynwood TN3 23 C2
Lyons Cres TN9 9 F3

Mabledon Rd TN9 8 D4
Macdonald Ct TN12 25 G4
Madeira Pk TN2 3 C6
Magnolia Cl TN9 9 F5
Magpie Grn TN8 29 C3
Maidstone Rd, Five Oak Green TN12 24 B6
Maidstone Rd, Hadlow TN11 7 E3
Maidstone Rd, Horsmonden TN12 26 B4
Maidstone Rd, Lower Green TN2 18 E2
Maidstone Rd, Paddock Wood TN12 25 F4
Main Rd TN8 29 B1
Major Yorks Rd TN4 3 A6
Mallard Way TN8 29 C3
Maltings Cl TN11 7 D3
Malton Way TN2 15 H5
Mann Sq TN9 9 G5
Manor Cl TN4 16 B2
Manor Gro TN10 9 F1
Manor House Gdns TN8 29 B5
Manor Pk TN4 16 B2
Manor Rd, Edenbridge TN8 29 B5
Manor Rd, Rusthall TN4 13 E5
Manor Rd, Southborough TN4 14 B2
Manor Way TN6 20 C6
Maple Cl TN2 16 C4
Mardens Hill TN6 20 A1
Market Pl TN2 3 A6
Market Sq TN1 3 D2
Market St TN2 3 D2
Marlborough Cl TN4 16 B1
Marlhurst TN8 29 B2
Marlpit Cl TN4 29 C2
Marlpit Gdns TN5 28 C5
Marsh Cl TN11 7 D2
Marshall Gdns TN11 7 D2
Martin Hardie Way TN10 6 A5
Marvillion Ct TN12 26 C2
Mary Magdalene Ho TN9 9 E4
Maryland Rd TN12 17 F4
Mascalls Court La TN12 25 H6
Mascalls Court Rd TN12 25 G5
Mascalls Pk TN12 25 F5
Masefield Way TN9 8 C5
Mayfield Cl TN20 23 A5
Mayfield La TN5 19 A4
Mayfield Rd TN5 19 C3
Mayfield Rd TN4 16 B1
Maylam Ct TN10 9 B5
Maynards Mead TN6 21 H6
Meadow Bank TN11 10 B2
Meadow Hill Rd TN11 3 C5
Meadow La TN8 29 B2
Meadow Rd, Groombridge TN3 23 C2
Meadow Rd, Rusthall TN4 13 E5
Meadow Rd, Southborough TN4 14 C2
Meadow Rd, Tonbridge TN9 9 E4
Meadow Rd, Tunbridge Wells TN1 3 C1
Meadowside TN5 28 D5
Meadway TN11 4 D5
Medina Rd TN10 5 G4
Medway TN6 21 F4
Medway Dr RH18 30 D2
Medway Mdws TN12 26 D2
Medway Rd TN1 15 E6
Medway Wharf Rd TN9 9 F3
Melfort Rd TN6 20 B5

Mendip Walk TN2 17 F1
Mercer St TN1 16 D1
Mercers, Cranbrook TN18 28 B2
Mercers, Tunbridge Wells TN3 13 C6
Mercers Cl TN12 25 F4
Mereworth Rd TN4 14 C5
Merlin Cl TN10 6 B6
Merrion Cl TN4 15 E4
Merrion Way TN4 15 E4
Merryfield Ct*, Quarry Gdns TN9 9 E4
Mersey Rd TN10 5 G5
Michael Flds RH18 30 B3
Middle Fld TN2 18 E2
Middle Garth TN17 27 C5
Middle Walk TN9 15 G4
Middlefield TN4 13 E5
Mill Bank TN9 9 F2
Mill Cres, Crowborough TN6 20 D3
Mill Cres, Tonbridge TN9 9 F2
Mill Dr TN6 20 D3
Mill Hill TN8 29 C6
Mill Hill Cotts TN8 29 C6
Mill La, Crowborough TN6 20 C4
Mill La, Tonbridge TN11 4 A3
Mill La, Tonbridge TN9 9 F2
Mill Stream Pl TN9 9 G2
Mill Vw TN11 7 C2
Millbrook Bsns Pk TN6 21 H6
Millbrook Ind Est TN6 21 H6
Millbrook Rd TN6 20 D4
Milton Dr TN2 15 F4
Milton Gdns TN9 8 C5
Mitre Ct TN9 9 F2
Moat Fm TN2 16 C6
Modesty Cotts TN4 14 A2
Moles Mead TN8 29 B4
Molescroft Way TN9 8 C5
Molyneux Ct TN4 16 B1
Molyneux Park Gdns TN4 3 A2
Molyneux Park Rd TN4 3 A2
Monks Walk*, Priory Walk TN9 9 E4
Monson Colonade*, Monson Rd TN1 3 C2
Monson Rd TN1 3 C2
Monson Way TN1 3 C3
Mont St Aignan Way TN8 29 C5
Montacute Gdns TN4 3 A6
Montacute Rd TN2 16 C4
Montargis Way TN6 20 D5
Monteith Cl TN3 13 D6
Montgomery Rd TN4 14 D4
Monypenny Cl TN11 7 C2
Morley Dr TN12 26 B4
Morley Rd TN9 9 G3
Mortley Cl TN9 9 F3
Mottins Hill TN6 22 F2
Mount Edgecombe Rd TN4 3 A4
Mount Ephraim TN1 3 A3
Mount Ephraim Ct TN1 3 A3
Mount Ephraim Rd TN1 3 B2
Mount Pleasant, Cranbrook TN18 28 A3
Mount Pleasant, Crowborough TN6 22 D2
Mount Pleasant, Hildenborough TN11 4 C4
Mount Pleasant, Paddock Wood TN12 25 F3
Mount Pleasant, Wadhurst TN5 19 D2
Mount Pleasant Av TN1 3 C3
Mount Pleasant Ct TN11 4 C4
Mount Pleasant Rd TN1 3 C4
Mount Sion TN1 3 B5
Mountfield Cl TN1 3 C4
Mountfield Gdns TN1 3 C4
Mountfield Pk TN9 9 F5
Mountfield Rd TN1 3 C4
Mulberry Cl TN4 21 E5
Munday Works Est TN9 9 F3
Murton Neale Cl TN18 28 C1
Myrtle Rd TN6 20 D5

Napier Rd TN2 17 F3
Nellington Rd TN4 12 D4
Nelson Av TN9 8 D3
Nelson Rd TN9 17 F3
Nevill Cl TN6 20 A6

Nevill Ct TN6 20 A6
Nevill Gate TN2 16 D4
Nevill Lodge*, Ferndale Cl TN1 17 E1
Nevill Pk TN4 16 A2
Nevill Rd TN6 20 D3
Nevill Ridge TN4 13 F6
Nevill St TN2 3 B6
Nevill Ter TN4 16 C4
New Bassetts Cotts TN12 26 C5
New Ct TN9 9 F2
New Dr TN3 23 B3
New England Rd TN4 14 D5
New Rd, Cranbrook TN17 27 A5
New Rd, Crowborough TN6 20 D3
New Rd, Tonbridge TN9 25 G4
New Wharf Rd TN9 9 E3
Newborough Ct TN6 5 H4
Newcombe Wood TN2 16 D5
Newcomen Rd TN4 14 C6
Newhouse Ter TN8 29 B3
Newick La TN20 23 B6
Newington Ct TN5 28 C5
Newlands TN3 13 D6
Newlands Pl RH18 30 C2
Newlands Rd TN4 14 D5
Newlands Rise TN4 14 D5
Newlands Way TN4 14 D4
Newton Av TN10 6 A3
Newton Gdns TN12 25 F3
Newton Rd TN1 3 C2
Newton Willows TN3 23 D2
Noble Tree Rd TN11 4 A4
Norbury Cl TN6 20 C2
Norfolk Heights TN1 3 B3
Norfolk Rd, Tonbridge TN9 8 D3
Norfolk Rd, Tunbridge Wells TN1 3 C5
Norman Rd TN1 3 D1
Norman Rise TN17 27 C6
Norris Cl TN18 28 C1
Norstead Gdns TN4 14 D4
North Beeches Rd TN6 21 E5
North Farm Ind Est TN2 15 F3
North Farm Rd TN2 15 E4
North Frith Pk TN11 6 B1
North St, Mayfield TN20 23 B3
North St, Tunbridge Wells TN2 17 E2
North Trench TN10 5 G4
Northcote Rd TN9 9 E4
Northdown Cl TN12 25 F3
Northfields TN3 12 C2
Northgrove Rd TN18 28 B1
Northwood Rd TN10 5 G4
Norton Cres TN10 5 G3
Norton Rd TN4 14 C2
Nortons Way TN12 24 B3
Norwich Av TN10 6 A6
Nottidge Rd TN4 16 A5
Nursery Cl TN10 6 A6
Nursery Rd, Tonbridge TN12 25 F2
Nursery Rd, Tunbridge Wells TN4 15 E3
Nye Cl TN2 20 D5

Oak End Cl TN4 14 C1
Oak Rd, Tonbridge TN12 24 B3
Oak Rd, Tunbridge Wells TN4 15 F4
Oak Ter*, Cranbrook Rd TN18 28 B1
Oak Tree Cl TN12 16 D4
Oak Vw TN8 29 B4
Oakdale Rd TN4 16 B1
Oakfield TN18 28 B1
Oakfield Ct TN2 17 E3
Oakfield Ct Rd TN2 17 E3
Oakfield Rd TN4 29 B1
Oakhurst Dr TN6 21 E3
Oakland Villas TN3 23 C2
Oaklands TN6 21 E5
Oaklands Rd, Cranbrook TN18 28 B2
Oaklands Rd, Tunbridge Wells TN3 23 C2
Oaklands Way TN11 5 E6
Oaklea Cl TN12 25 G4
Oakmead TN10 5 H4
Oakwood Pk RH18 30 C3
Oakwood Rise TN2 15 G3
Oast Cl TN2 16 A6

Oast La TN10 5 F6
Oast Vw TN12 26 B5
Oatfield Cl TN17 27 B4
Oatfield Dr TN17 27 B4
Ockley La TN18 28 B1
Ockley Rd TN18 28 B1
Old Barn Cl TN9 8 D4
Old Cannon Wharf TN9 9 G3
Old Gardens Cl TN12 16 D5
Old Hadlow Rd TN10 6 B6
Old Kent Rd TN12 25 G4
Old La, Crowborough TN6 20 B3
Old La, Mayfield TN20 23 A5
Old La, Poundfield TN6 21 F5
Old London Rd TN10 9 F1
Old Mill Ct TN6 20 C4
Old Rd TN12 26 C2
Old Station Rd TN5 19 D1
Oliver Cl TN6 21 E5
Orchard Bsns Centre, Tonbridge TN9 9 H3
Orchard Bsns Centre, Tunbridge Wells TN2 15 F3
Orchard Cl, Crowborough TN6 22 B1
Orchard Cl, Edenbridge TN8 29 A4
Orchard Cl, Tonbridge TN12 26 A4
Orchard Cl, Tunbridge Wells TN1 5 F5
Orchard Cres TN12 26 B4
Orchard Dr, Edenbridge TN8 29 A4
Orchard Dr, Tonbridge TN10 6 B5
Orchard Lea TN11 5 E5
Orchard Rd TN12 26 C2
Orchard Rise TN3 23 B2
Orchard Way, Cranbrook TN17 27 A6
Orchard Way, Tonbridge TN12 26 B4
Orchidhurst TN2 15 F4
Osborne Hill TN6 21 G6
Osborne Rd TN6 21 G6
Osmers Hill TN5 19 E1
Osmunda Ct*, Ferndale Cl TN1 17 E1
Ospringe Pl TN2 15 H6
Ox Lea TN3 13 D6
Oxfield TN8 29 C3

Paddock Wood Distribution Centre TN12 25 H2
Palesgate La TN6 21 F2
Palmers Brook TN11 7 E1
Park Av, Edenbridge TN8 29 B4
Park Av, Tonbridge TN11 5 E5
Park Cotts TN18 28 C1
Park Cres, Crowborough TN6 20 D3
Park Cres, Forest Row RH18 30 D3
Park House Gdns TN4 14 C2
Park La TN6 20 D3
Park Rd, Crowborough TN6 20 D3
Park Rd, Forest Row RH18 30 D3
Park Rd, Southborough TN4 14 C1
Park Rd, Tunbridge Wells TN4 14 D6
Park St TN2 17 E2
Park View Cl TN6 29 B4
Park Villas TN11 7 E2
Parklands TN4 14 B3
Parkway TN10 6 A5
Parkwood Cl TN2 15 F5
Parsonage Ct TN4 12 E4
Parsonage Rd TN4 13 E5
Pattenden Gdns TN12 26 D1
Peach Hall TN10 5 H4
Pear Tree Cl TN17 27 C6
Peckham Ct TN12 26 C2
Pell Cl TN5 19 F1
Pell Hill TN5 19 F2
Pellings Farm Cl TN6 21 E3
Pellings Rise TN6 21 E3
Pemble Cl TN12 24 B3
Pembroke Rd TN9 8 D3
Pembury Cl TN2 18 D3
Pembury Grange TN2 18 A3

Pembury Gro TN9 9 F4
Pembury Rd, Pembury TN11 18 A1
Pembury Rd, Tonbridge TN9 9 E4
Pembury Rd, Tunbridge Wells TN2 17 E2
Pen Way TN10 6 B5
Pendrill Pl TN5 19 E2
Penfolds Cl TN10 5 H5
Penlee Cl TN8 29 C4
Pennine Walk TN2 17 F1
Pennington Pl TN4 14 D1
Pennington Rd TN4 14 C1
Pennyfields TN17 27 C4
Penshurst Rd, Leigh TN11 10 A2
Penshurst Rd, Penshurst TN3,11 10 A4
Penshurst Rd, Speldhurst TN3,11 12 A1
Percy Ter TN4 14 C5
Petersfield TN2 18 E2
Philpots La TN11 4 A4
Piccadilly La TN11 23 D6
Pickforde La TN5 28 B5
Pilmer Rd TN6 20 D3
Pine Gro, Crowborough TN6 20 C4
Pine Gro, Edenbridge TN8 29 B4
Pine Ridge TN10 5 G4
Pinewood Chase TN6 20 B3
Pinewood Cl TN12 25 G4
Pinewood Ct TN4 14 C2
Pinewood Gdns TN4 14 C2
Pinewood Rd TN2 15 F6
Pink Alley TN2 3 A6
Pinkham TN12 26 C3
Pinkham Gdns TN12 26 C3
Pipers Cl TN5 19 F3
Pippin Rd TN12 26 B2
Pit La TN8 29 B2
Pittswood Cotts TN11 6 D2
Plane Walk TN10 5 H3
Pleasant View Rd TN6 20 C2
Plough Walk TN8 29 C3
Plover Cl TN8 29 C3
Polesden Rd TN2 17 F3
Polley Cl TN2 18 D3
Pollington Pl TN6 20 D4
Poona Rd TN1 3 D5
Poppy Mdw TN12 25 H4
Portland Cl TN10 6 A3
Portman Pk TN9 9 F1
Post Horn Cl RH18 30 E4
Post Horn La RH18 30 E3
Post Office Rd TN18 28 B1
Postern La TN11 9 G3
Pound Rd TN12 26 B1
Poundfield Fm TN6 21 F4
Poundfield Rd TN6 21 E4
Poundsbridge Hill TN3 12 A2
Powder Mill La, Leigh TN11 10 B2
Powder Mill La, Powder Mills TN11 8 B2
Powder Mill La, Tunbridge Wells TN4 14 D4
Powdermill Cl TN4 15 E3
Pratts Folly La TN6 20 C5
Preston Rd TN9 8 D3
Priestley Dr TN10 6 A3
Primmers Green Rd TN5 19 E2
Primrose La RH18 30 D3
Primrose Walk TN12 25 G5
Princes St TN2 17 E2
Priory Gro TN9 9 E4
Priory Rd, Forest Row RH18 30 A4
Priory Rd, Tonbridge TN9 9 E4
Priory St TN9 9 E4
Priory Walk TN9 9 E4
Prospect Pk TN4 14 B2
Prospect Rd, Southborough TN4 14 B2
Prospect Rd, Tunbridge Wells TN2 3 D5
Providence Cotts TN3 23 C1
Purcell Av TN10 6 C5
Puttenden Rd TN11 6 B1

Quaker Dr TN17 27 C3
Quaker La TN17 27 C3
Quantock Cl TN2 17 F1
Quarry Bank TN9 8 D5
Quarry Cotts TN5 19 C1
Quarry Gdns TN9 9 E4

Quarry Hill Par*,
  High St TN9 9 E4
Quarry Hill Rd TN9 8 D6
Quarry Rd TN1 15 E6
Quarry Rise TN9 8 D5
Queens Cotts TN5 19 D2
Queens Ct,
  Cranbrook TN18 28 C1
Queens Ct,
  Edenbridge TN8 29 C5
Queens Gdns TN4 14 D5
Queens Mws TN18 28 C1
Queens Rd,
  Cranbrook TN18 28 C1
Queens Rd,
  Crowborough TN6 20 D6
Queens Rd,
  Tunbridge Wells TN4 14 D5
Quincewood Gdns TN10 5 G3

Raeburn Cl TN10 6 B4
Rammell Mws TN17 27 C5
Ramslye Rd TN4 16 A5
Rankine Rd TN2 15 F4
Rannoch Rd TN4 20 B4
Rannoch Rd West TN6 20 B4
Raphael Ct TN11 4 D3
Ravenswood Av TN2 15 F6
Rectory Dr TN3 10 D4
Rectory Flds TN17 27 C4
Rectory La TN17 27 C4
Redbridge La TN6 22 A3
Redpoll Walk TN12 25 G5
Redwood Pk TN12 24 A4
Regency Hall TN2 3 A6
Regent Pl TN2 17 F2
Regina Ct TN4 16 B2
Rembrandt Cl TN10 6 B4
Reynolds Cl TN10 6 A4
Reynolds La TN4 14 B5
Ribston Gdns TN12 25 F3
Richardson Rd TN4 14 D6
Richmead Gdns TN20 23 B5
Richmond Pl TN2 16 D5
Riddlesdale Av TN4 14 D5
Ridge Way TN8 29 C2
Ridgelands TN3 10 D4
Ridgeway TN2 18 D2
Ridgeway Cres TN10 6 A6
Riding La TN11 4 C1
Riding Pk TN11 4 C3
Ringden Av TN12 25 F4
Rings Hill TN11 4 A6
River Lawn Rd TN9 9 E3
River Walk TN9 9 E3
Riverdale Ind Est TN9 9 G4
Riverside,
  Edenbridge TN8 29 C5
Riverside,
  Forest Row RH18 30 B2
Riverside Centre TN9 9 F3
Riverside Ct,
  Edenbridge TN8 29 C5
Riverside Ct,
  Tonbridge TN9 9 F3
Riverside Gdns TN6 21 G6
Robin Cl TN12 25 G5
Robyns Way TN8 29 C6
Rochdale Rd TN1 15 E6
Rochester Ho TN6 21 G5
Rochester Rd TN10 6 A6
Rochester Way TN6 21 F5
Rochmans Way TN6 21 E6
Rock Villa Rd TN1 3 B2
Rockington Way TN6 21 F5
Rodmell Rd TN2 16 C4
Rodney Av TN10 6 B6
Rodwell TN6 21 G5
Roedean Heights TN2 16 D4
Roedean Rd TN2 16 C4
Romford Rd TN2 18 E3
Romney Way TN10 6 A5
Rookley Cl TN2 17 F3
Roopers TN3 12 C2
Rope Walk TN17 27 B4
Ropers Gate TN4 16 B4
Rose St TN9 9 F4
Rosecroft Pk TN3 13 C5
Rosehill Gdns TN6 21 G5
Rosehill Walk TN1 3 B3
Roselands Av TN20 23 A6
Rossdale TN2 15 F6
Rother Cl TN6 22 B2
Rother Rd TN10 5 G5
Rotherfield La TN20 23 A4
Rotherfield Rd TN6 21 H6
Rotherhill Rd TN6 22 B2

Rothermead TN20 23 A6
Roundhill Rd TN2 17 F5
Rowan Cl TN12 25 F4
Rowan Shaw TN10 5 H4
Rowan Tree Rd TN6 16 B4
Rowfield TN8 29 C3
Royal Av TN9 9 F4
Royal Chase TN4 3 A1
Royal Oak Mws TN20 23 B4
Royal Rise TN9 9 F4
Royal Tunbridge Wells
  Bsns Pk TN2 15 G2
Royal Victoria Pl
  Shopping Centre TN1 3 C2
Royal West Kent Av TN10 5 H6
Ruffets Ct TN4 16 A4
Ruscombe Cl TN4 14 C1
Rushetts TN3 14 C3
Russell Mews TN12 25 F3
Russells Yd TN17 27 C5
Russett Rd TN12 26 B7
Rusthall Grange TN4 13 F5
Rusthall High St TN4 13 E5
Rusthall Pk TN4 16 A2
Rusthall Rd TN4 13 F5
Rustwick TN4 16 A1
Rutherford Way TN10 14 A6
Rydal Cl TN4 14 A6
Rydal Dr TN4 14 A6
Ryders TN3 13 C6
Rye Rd TN18 28 B2
Rymers Cl TN2 15 F4
Ryst Wood Rd RH18 30 E3

St Andrews Cl TN12 25 G3
St Andrews Ct TN4 14 C2
St Andrews Park Rd TN4 14 C2
St Andrews Rd TN12 25 G4
St Barnabas Cl TN1 15 E6
St Bernards Rd TN10 14 D6
St Brelades Ct TN8 29 A3
St Davids Rd TN4 14 C5
St Denys Vw TN6 21 E5
St Dunstans Walk TN17 27 C5
St Georges Mws*,
  George St TN9 9 E4
St Georges Pk TN2 16 C5
St James Cl TN10 6 A3
St James Ct TN1 3 D1
St James Pk TN1 15 E6
St James Rd TN1 15 E6
St Johns Cl TN6 20 C3
St Johns Rd TN4 14 C3
St Johns Rd,
  Crowborough TN6 20 B2
St Johns Rd,
  Tunbridge Wells TN4 14 C6
St Lawrence Av TN4 11 E4
St Lukes Rd TN4 14 D5
St Marks Rd TN2 16 B6
St Mary-in-the-Fields
  TN20 23 B5
St Marys Cl TN5 28 B5
St Marys La,
  Tunbridge Wells TN3 12 C2
St Marys La,
  Wadhurst TN5 28 B5
St Marys Rd TN9 9 E5
St Michaels Cl TN6 21 F6
St Michaels Ct TN11 4 C3
St Michaels Rd TN4 14 D5
St Pauls Cl TN6 6 A5
St Pauls Rd TN4 13 E5
St Peters St TN2 17 E2
St Richards Rd TN6 22 C2
St Stephens Cotts*,
  Stanley Rd TN4 14 D6
St Stephens St TN9 9 E4
St Thomas of
  Canterbury Ct TN20 23 B5
Salisbury Cl TN10 6 A5
Salisbury Rd,
  High Brooms TN4 15 E3
Salisbury Rd,
  Langton Green TN3 13 B6
Salisbury Rd,
  Tonbridge TN9 9 F3
Salomons Rd TN4 13 F5
Sanderson Way TN9 9 G3
Sandhurst Av TN2 18 E4
Sandhurst Cl TN2 15 F5
Sandhurst Pk TN2 15 F4
Sandhurst Rd TN2 15 E4
Sandown Cl TN2 15 H5
Sandown Gro TN2 15 H5
Sandown Pk TN2 15 H5
Sandridge TN6 20 C5
Sandringham Mews TN4 14 D6

Sandrock Ho*,
  Sandrock Rd TN2 17 F1
Sandrock Rd TN2 17 E1
Saunders Rd TN4 16 A5
Saville Cl TN10 6 A3
Saxby Wood TN11 10 A2
Saxbury Cl TN6 20 D4
School Fld TN8 29 B4
School La,
  Crowborough TN6 20 D5
School La,
  Forest Row RH18 30 C3
School La,
  St Johns TN6 20 B2
School La,
  Tonbridge TN11 7 D3
School Rise TN6 16 B5
School Ter TN18 28 B1
Scott Rd TN9 8 C5
Scotts Way TN2 16 B5
Seabrook Rd TN6 8 D1
Sefton Chase TN6 21 E3
Sefton Way TN6 21 E3
Senlac Pl TN3 23 C1
Severn Cl TN10 5 H5
Shaftesbury Rd TN4 14 C6
Shakespeare Rd TN8 8 C5
Shalesbrook La RH18 30 D4
Shandon Cl TN2 17 E2
Shawfield TN6 21 F4
Sheaffe Dr TN17 27 B4
Sheep Plain TN6 20 B6
Sheffield Rd TN4 14 C1
Sheiling Rd TN6 20 C3
Shelton Cl TN10 5 H5
Shepherds Walk,
  Crowborough TN6 21 F5
Shepherds Walk,
  Tunbridge Wells TN2 17 F2
Sherborne La TN2 17 G3
Sheridan Ct TN10 5 E6
Sherwood Rd TN2 15 F5
Sherwood Way TN2 15 G5
Shipbourne Rd TN10,11 5 H6
Shirley Cotts*,
  Woodbury Park Rd TN4 14 D6
Shirley Gdns TN4 12 F4
Shirley Gro TN4 12 F4
Showfields Rd TN2 16 B5
Shrublands Ct,
  Tonbridge TN9 9 F2
Shrublands Ct,
  Tunbridge Wells TN2 17 E1
Sidney Cl TN2 16 B5
Silver Cl TN9 9 E6
Silverdale Rd TN4 15 E5
Silverdale Rd TN4 15 E5
Silverhurst Dr TN10 5 H4
Silwood Cl TN2 15 G5
Simons Cl TN6 21 E5
Sir Davids Pk TN4 14 B3
Siskin Gdns TN12 25 G5
Six Penny Cl TN8 29 C5
Skeynes Rd TN8 29 B5
Skinners La TN8 29 C3
Skinners Ter TN9 9 E4
Slip Mill Rd TN18 28 A1
Smithers Cl TN11 7 D2
Smithers Ct TN12 26 D1
Smithers La TN12 26 D1
Smithyfield TN8 29 D3
Smugglers TN18 28 C2
Smugglers La TN6 20 B1
Smythe Cl TN5 11 F5
Snape Vw TN5 19 E4
Snipe Cl TN2 18 E2
Snoll Hatch Rd TN12 26 B3
Somerhill Rd TN9 9 G4
Somerset Rd TN4 14 C5
Somerset Villas TN3 23 C1
Somerville Gdns TN4 3 A2
Sopers La TN18 28 A1
Sorrell Cl TN8 29 C3
South Gro TN1 3 B5
South St,
  Crowborough TN6 20 D5
South St, Mayfield TN20 23 B5
South St, Mayfield TN20 23 C5
South View Rd,
  Tunbridge Wells TN4 15 E4
South View Rd,
  Wadhurst TN5 19 E2
Southfield Rd TN4 14 C5
Southfields,
  Tunbridge Wells TN3 12 C2
Southfields,
  Wadhurst TN5 19 E1
Southfields Way TN4 14 D4

Southgate TN4 16 B2
Southmead Cl TN20 23 D4
Southridge Rd TN6 20 C6
Southridge Rise TN6 20 C6
Southview Rd TN6 20 B6
Southway Cl TN6 20 C5
Southway Av TN4 14 D5
Southwood Rd TN4 12 E4
Sovereign Way TN9 9 F3
Spa Cl TN11 7 E2
Spa Ind Pk TN2 15 G3
Sparrows Grn Rd TN6 19 E3
Sparrows Grn*,
  Sparrows Green Rd TN5 19 E2
Speedwell Cl TN8 29 C2
Speldhurst Hill TN3 12 D2
Speldhurst Rd,
  Langton Green TN3 13 B6
Speldhurst Rd,
  Southborough TN3 14 C2
Spelmonden Rd TN12 26 A6
Spencer Mws,
  Berkeley Rd TN1 3 B5
Spencer Mws,
  Camden Rd TN1 3 D2
Speyside TN10 5 G5
Spring Gdns TN4 13 E5
Spring La TN3 10 D5
Spring Mdw RH18 30 C4
Springfield Cl TN6 21 F4
Springfield Ind Est
  TN18 28 B1
Springfield Pl TN3 23 C1
Springfield Rd,
  Edenbridge TN8 29 B5
Springfield Rd,
  Groombridge TN3 23 C2
Springfield Rd,
  Southborough TN4 14 C2
Springfields TN5 28 C5
Springhead TN2 15 F6
Springhead Way TN6 20 C6
Springwell Rd TN9 9 E5
Springwood Pk TN11 6 A2
Squirrel Way TN2 17 G1
Stabledene Way TN8 18 D4
Staces Cotts TN12 25 F5
Stacey Rd TN10 5 E6
Stackfield TN8 29 C3
Stafford Cl TN2 17 G1
Stafford Rd TN3 9 E2
Stag Rd TN2 15 G3
Stainer Rd TN10 6 B4
Stair Rd TN10 6 C6
Stanam Rd TN2 18 E4
Stanbridge Rd TN8 29 B4
Standen St TN4 14 C6
Stangrove Ct TN8 29 B4
Stangrove Rd TN8 29 B5
Stanhope Rd TN1 15 E6
Stanley Rd TN1 14 D6
Star La TN20 23 C5
Star Mws TN20 23 B5
Starfield TN6 20 C5
Station App,
  Edenbridge TN8 29 C4
Station App,
  Mayfield TN20 23 A5
Station App,
  Tonbridge TN12 25 G3
Station Cotts TN12 26 C5
Station Rd,
  Crowborough TN6 21 G6
Station Rd,
  Edenbridge TN8 29 B2
Station Rd,
  Forest Row RH18 30 C2
Station Rd,
  Mayfield TN20 23 A5
Station Rd,
  Tonbridge TN3 23 C2
Station Rd,
  Tunbridge Wells TN3 23 C2
Station Rd,
  Wadhurst TN5 19 A1
Steellands Rise TN5 28 C5
Steep Rd TN6 22 D3
Steers Pl TN11 7 D1
Stephens Rd TN4 14 D6
Stewart Rd TN4 15 E4
Still La TN4 14 C1
Stockenbury TN12 26 B3
Stockland Green Rd TN3 12 E2
Stocks Green Rd TN11 4 A6
Stone Court La TN2 18 E2
Stone Cross TN20 23 A5
Stone Cross Rd,
  Crowborough TN6 22 B3

Stone Cross Rd,
  Wadhurst TN5 19 F4
Stone St,
  Cranbrook TN17 27 C4
Stone St,
  Tunbridge Wells TN1 3 D1
Stonebridge La TN5 19 D1
Stonecott Ct TN6 20 D6
Stonedene Cl RH18 30 E3
Stonepark Dr RH18 30 E3
Stonewall Park Rd TN3 13 B6
Stonewood Cl TN4 14 C3
Stoneyfield TN8 29 C3
Stour Cl TN10 5 G5
Stratford St TN1 15 E6
Strawberry Cl TN2 16 A6
Strawberry Vale TN9 9 F4
Stream Side TN10 6 A3
Streatfield TN8 29 C5
Strettitt Gdns TN12 26 C3
Stuart Cl TN2 16 B5
Styles Ct TN12 25 G3
Suffolk Mews TN1 3 B3
Sullivan Rd TN10 6 B5
Summerhill Av TN4 14 B2
Summervale Rd TN4 16 A4
Sunhill Ct TN2 18 C4
Sunnybank Cl TN20 23 C5
Sunnyside TN8 29 B2
Sunnyside Rd TN4 13 F5
Surrey Cl TN2 16 B5
Sussex Cl TN2 17 E4
Sussex Mws TN2 3 A6
Sussex Rd TN9 8 D4
Sutherland Rd TN1 3 C5
Swallow Dr TN2 15 H5
Swan La TN8 29 B2
Swan Ridge TN8 29 C2
Swanland Dr TN9 8 C5
Swanmead Way TN9 9 G2
Swans Ghyll RH18 30 B2
Swaylands Av TN6 22 B2
Sweeps Hill Cl TN2 18 D3
Swift Cl TN6 20 B5
Swifts Vw TN17 27 C3
Sybron Way TN6 21 H6
Sycamore Cotts TN2 18 C4
Sycamore Gdns TN12 25 G5
Sychem La TN12 24 B3
Sychem Pl TN12 24 A3

Tabor Ct*,
  Maidstone Rd TN12 26 B4
Tainter Rd TN11 7 D2
Talbot Pk TN2 15 F6
Talbot Rd TN18 28 A3
Tamar Rd TN10 5 G5
Tanners Mead TN8 29 B5
Tanners Way TN6 21 E5
Tannery Rd TN9 9 F3
Tanyard Hill TN3 23 C3
Tapsells La TN5 19 B2
Tarbutts TN17 27 F3
Tarland Ho TN2 17 F3
Tates TN18 28 B2
Taylor Ct*,
  Brook Rd TN2 15 F4
Taylor St TN4 14 C3
Tea Garden La TN3 13 E6
Tedder Rd TN4 14 D4
Teise Cl TN2 17 F3
Templars Ct TN8 29 C3
Thames Rd TN10 5 G5
The Avenue,
  Mayfield TN20 23 C5
The Avenue,
  Tonbridge TN9 9 E2
The Beeches TN2 15 F6
The Bines TN12 25 G5
The Birches TN9 13 E6
The Boundary TN3 13 E6
The Brent TN10 5 H4
The Cedars TN12 25 G3
The Chase,
  Tonbridge TN9 5 G5
The Chase,
  Tunbridge Wells TN2 3 D5
The Cherry Orch TN11 7 D2
The Chestnuts TN18 28 A3
The Close,
  Crowborough TN6 20 C3
The Close,
  Tunbridge Wells TN3 23 C2
The Colonnade TN18 28 B1
The Coppice TN2 18 D3
The Crescent,
  Cranbrook TN17 27 C5